FUNNY
The Book
Everything You Always Wanted to Know About Comedy

David Misch

APPLAUSE
THEATRE & CINEMA BOOKS

AN IMPRINT OF
HAL•LEONARD®

Published in 2012 by Applause Theater & Cinema Books
An Imprint of Hal Leonard Corporation
7777 West Bluemound Road
Milwaukee, WI 53213

Trade Book Division Editorial Offices
33 Plymouth St., Montclair, NJ 07042

Printed in the United States of America
Book design by Mark Lerner

Library of Congress Cataloging-in-Publication Data

Misch, David.
 Funny the book : everything you always wanted to know about comedy / David Misch.
    p. cm.
1. Wit and humor--History and criticism. 2. Comedy--History and criticism. 3. Comic, The. I. Title.
PN6147.M527 2012
809.7
                              2012002359

ISBN 978-1-55783-829-2

www.applausebooks.com

For Amy and Emily, whose laughter makes me happy

CONTENTS

ACKNOWLEDGMENTS

**In order of height and vocal timbre;
beginning with 5′11″, light tenor ...**

Bob Weide—for "From which direction?"
Julia Lord—for selling me
Andrew Post—for Edshu
Adele Lander Burke—for legitimizing me
Gordon Mitchell—for "It Worked on *Cheers*"
Lily Bergman—for the title
Buddy Morra—for managing me
Peggy Sarlin—for suggesting I write a book
Nora Glasner—for indexing
John Cerullo—for buying the first copy
Marybeth Keating—for shepherding
Monique Thomas—for the Penis Festival
Jill Jonnes—for helping with being an author
Tom Lehrer—for "Vatican Rag"

For Being Good People

Lee Kalcheim
Ellis Weiner
Jeff Reno
Ron Osborn
Victoria Zackheim
David Leaf
Larry Cutler
David Sonne
Michael Silverblatt
Jason Alexander
Danny Klein
Maryedith Burrell

For USC

Elizabeth Daley
Jack Epps Jr.
Barnet Kellman
David Isaacs
Hedwin Naimark

For Photos

Cheryl Van Grunsven—finding
Kate Coe—getting
Bob Carlsen—fixing
Bernard Kane—helping

Funny: The Book

Introduction

Guy goes to a doctor, doctor says, "You're gonna die." Guy says, "Oh my god! How long do I have?" "10." "10 what?! Weeks? Months?" "9 . . . 8 . . ."

There are two human activities that result in physical pleasure so intense that it produces a series of helpless, high-pitched vocal spasms.

You've chosen a book about the one that uses fart jokes.

Of course, comedy's a lot more than that. Yet the closer we look, the more mysterious it becomes.

It started out simply enough; in ancient Greece, a comedy ended with a wedding, tragedy

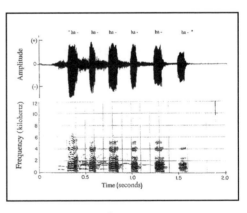

Spasm

with a funeral. (But remember, you can't spell *funeral* without *fun*.) Thousands of years later, Mel Brooks declared, "Tragedy is when I cut my finger; comedy is when you walk into an open sewer and die." Still, the differences resist easy categorization. Jerry Lewis said comedy is a man in trouble; okay, so what's drama?

Rodney Dangerfield told this joke: "I go to a bar, bartender asks, 'What'll you have?' I say, 'Surprise me.' So he shows me a naked picture of my wife."

Surprise is the key to humor ("Peekaboo!" is everyone's first comedy routine), but surprise is the key to all art and entertainment; it's what makes a story gripping, a ballet thrilling, a painting unforgettable.* So how is comedy different?

Please note this admission does not entitle you to a refund, but I don't know.

No one knows why putting one particular word at the end of a sentence makes that sentence funny rather than sad. (Or two words in the case of "in bed.") When we describe how humor works, we describe how all art forms work—there is no principle of comedy that doesn't also apply to drama.

So why investigate comedy at all? Why try to discover its secret? Why not just leave it alone in its ethnic-joked, pie-splattered mystery?

Because, as a wise man has written, "Humor is an essential element of human identity." ** Knowledge of the principles and practice of comedy is critical to understanding history, psychology, mass media, religion, and real estate investment. (One of those is a lie.)

E. B. White, author of *Charlotte's Web*, thought examining comedy was futile. "Humor can be dissected as a frog can," he wrote, "but the thing dies in the process and the innards are discouraging to any but the pure scientific mind." Well, who's he to talk—the spider died, how funny is that?

If dissecting a discipline killed enjoyment, no one would study anything they liked. Yes, explaining a joke can make it not funny,

---

* And not just art and entertainment—Ron Graham, president of the American Mathematical Society: "What makes a mathematical result beautiful or a proof elegant is the element of surprise."
** Misch: *Funny: The Book*, 2012, p. 1.

but nonstop yucks isn't the goal of this book. (Assuming you don't have the copy embedded with laughing gas on page 8.) It's to look at humor in general and American humor in particular; introduce/ remind and/or get you to think about significant works; and show how American comedy developed out of what Martin Luther King called, in a slightly different context, the content of our characters. We'll discuss the origins, definition, rules, and purpose of comedy, and what it tells us about the human condition. In bed.

So let the dissection begin!

My examples won't necessarily be the best or even the most representative, just the ones I'm most interested in. And some will be old. Why? Guy reads *Hamlet* for the first time; friend asks, "How'd you like it?"; guy says, "It's nothing but a bunch of quotations." When you know the foundations of comedy, contemporary movies and TV shows are huge heaping bowlsful of quotations; this book will talk about the originals.

From time to time, the author will project through these pages, using only the power of his mind, examples of humor that illustrate his points. For those unable to receive these projections, links are provided at the end of this book (in a section cunningly entitled "Links") for viewing these examples over the far-flung series of tubes we call the Interwebs.

Speaking of which, due to ~~the skinflint lily-livered publisher refusing to spring for a coffee-table tome that could have made me rich beyond my wildest dreams~~ technical considerations, this book doesn't include interactive media. But for the most part I'm not a fan of what the Internet calls user-generated content, which gets most of its comedy from being "real." A laugh is a laugh, I accept that, but art isn't real, it's *artificial*. And it's not democratic—it's elitist, created by someone who uses special skills to alter reality and, in doing so, reveal some higher form of truth. (Hey, I just defined *artist*!)

Still, while accepting the cruciality of professional standards underpinning the creation of art and entertainment, I have to admit a cat flushing a toilet is funny . . .

See link 1: Glorious medley of cats flushing toilets to the unforget-table melody "It's a cat / flushing the toilet."

Finally, because the subject of Humor is so vast, by necessity this treatise will be half-vast.

And that is one of three puns in this book.

1

The History of Ha!

TRICKSTER

Socrates, Aristophanes, and Agathon were drinking out of a large goblet and Socrates was discoursing to them. Aristodemus was only half-awake and did not hear the beginning of the discourse; the chief thing he remembered was Socrates compelling the others to acknowledge that the genius of Comedy was the same with that of Tragedy. To this they were constrained to assent, being drowsy and not quite following the argument.

—Plato, *The Symposium*

People have been not quite following the argument for twenty-four hundred years now. When the closest an entire art form gets to respect is a few drunk philosophers saying "Sure, whatever, comedy's great, can I go to bed now?," I figure it's time to make the argument clearer.

Funny: The Early Years

Humor was probably invented by a Neanderthal who tripped over a log to amuse his cavemates, then fell into the fire and burned to death, thereby inventing irony as well.

Ironic

But what may seem like a quirk in our makeup is actually an essential element of human identity. (See, I told you.*)

From its beginnings, which we can guess were a kind of instinctive response, to the point where it was used deliberately to further our goals as a species, humor has been critical for humanity's survival and, perhaps as importantly, our need to do more than just survive.

While there's no record of the beginnings of comedy, we do have some first-hand observations from a 2000 Year Old Man, miraculously still alive in the person of Mel Brooks, here quizzed by Carl Reiner about life in prehistoric times . . .

See link 2: Brooks explains that the primary means of propulsion in Prehistory was "fear"; and that he's been married several hundred times, has "42,000 children . . . and not one comes to visit."

Trickster

Uproarious, chaotic, bad taste—all terms that have been used about Brooks and his comedy . . . and a figure known as Trickster, who began as mythology and became flesh in tribal ceremonies and rituals around the globe. Part human, part animal, part divine; part hero, part buffoon—Trickster first emerges in cave paintings eighteen thousand

---

* This is a reference to the introduction. If you skipped the introduction, it's an obscure in-joke.

years ago (warriors don't appear until nine thousand years later, and *South Park* many years after that).

The word "Trickster" is a modern construct; historians and anthropologists still debate its meaning, and he (Tricksters are almost always men) goes by many names:

Anansi (Haiti/West Africa)
Br'er Rabbit, Signifying Monkey (African American)
Bamapana (Australia, Aborigine)
Changó (Afro-Cuban)
Coyote (Native American)
Curupira (Brazil)
Harlequin (from Italian opera to Picasso) (Europe)
Hershel Ostropoler (Jewish)
Hitar Petar (Bulgaria)
Huehuecoyotl (Aztec)
Ivan the Fool (Russia)
Kagen (Bushmen)
Kitsune (Japan)
Krishna, Mohini (female) (Hindu)
Leprechauns (Ireland)
Monkey King (China)
Nasreddin (Persia)
Raven (Inuits)
Renart the Fox (France)
Robin Goodfellow (England)
Taliesen (Wales)
Til Uilenspiegel (Germany/Holland)
Uncle Tompa (Tibet)

Different though they are, Tricksters all share three key features:

☞ *Exaggerated sexuality*: Some, like the Greek Trickster-messenger Hermes, are depicted with outsized erections (though of course, the definition of "outsized" is open to interpretation) (I'm talking to you, Wife #2).

☞ *Existential ambivalence*: Tricksters often live in a no-man's land between the human and the divine—think Shakespeare's Puck.

☞ *Love for mischief*, based on inverting the status quo—think Brooks.

Trickster upends society through a myriad of methods: insulting the powerful, con games, practical jokes. He plays with people by playing with words, using puns, double-entendres, malaprops, tongue twisters, oxymorons. Henry Louis Gates Jr. says Trickster "dwells at the margins of discourse, ever punning, ever troping, ever embodying the ambiguities of language."

And why? Primarily, just for the hell of it. Gates quotes a "toast" about a famous African Trickster: "Deep down in the jungle, so they say/There's a signifying monkey down the way./There'd been no disturbin' in the jungle for quite a bit/So up jumped the monkey and laughed 'Guess I'll start some shit.'"

But Trickster isn't always anarchic; his stories can have a pointed purpose beneath the surface—for American slaves, Br'er Rabbit outwitting his stronger nemesis, Br'er Fox, went beyond entertainment to become a symbol of hope.

Whatever the culture, Trickster tales reveal humankind's infinite capacity for gall, gullibility, and greed; they show, as one of literature's trickiest Tricksters said, "What fools these mortals be." They touch on our greatest questions; scholar Lewis Hyde says Trickster breaks down distinctions between wisdom and folly, rule and disorder, to expose the unknowable mysteries of existence.

While not sacred himself, Trickster is often portrayed as essential to creation, or birth, playing an important part in early mythologies and rituals. But why give a central ceremonial role to a comedic character? (Note, for example, the relative dearth of wackiness in Catholicism.)

One theory is that primitive societies recognized—at a visceral rather than intellectual level—that the sacred was revealed through upset, reversal, surprise. Since those qualities are, as we'll see, fundamental to humor, maybe they thought laughter helped open the mind and heart to nonlogical, transcendent experience.

Or maybe Trickster was used to teach lessons, often by counterexample, making him almost a parody of the shaman (the wise and powerful teacher/healer/magician)—his earthy, secular, mischievous counterpart.

Or maybe Trickster represents memories of a past where there was no clear-cut distinction between the sacred and the profane. Carl Jung said Trickster "is a forerunner of the savior and, like him, God, man and animal at once." Perhaps the nearest contemporary equivalent is George Clooney.

Jung's definition fits what anthropologists call the *culture hero*, a middle being in religious evolution who exists between the animal spirit and God, and who, through the centuries, develops into God.

Some say Trickster's travels between base existence and the ethereal realm mirror the eternal but hopeless desire of our limited minds to explain the universe. Which is the human condition: we're all limited beings who want to know what the hell's going on.

While the specifics of his role varied by civilization and culture, Trickster seems to both mediate and celebrate the divide between human and divine, individual and society, meaning and absurdity.

All of which are in constant flux. Because if there's one thing in life that never changes, it's that everything changes. And Trickster, in upending society, forcing it to reexamine its values, is a key part of that perpetual process of protean permutation.

Nice Alliteration but I Thought This Was Gonna Be Funny

Don't worry—fart jokes ahead.

Jung believed Trickster was a manifestation of the collective unconscious. (Of course, he believed that about everything.) Interestingly, psychologists have found traditional qualities of Trickster in schizophrenics, which suggests he's potentially inside all of us, straddling the murky border between sanity and madness.

Borders are key to Trickster mythology: Èlegba, or Edshu, a shapeshifter from Nigeria's Yoruba tribe, has no home and exists at the crossroads, or the edge of someone's property—anywhere boundaries are unclear or disputed.

There are ancient Greek cups that got ancient Greek laughs from decorations showing satyrs (another incarnation of Trickster) trying to have sex with everything on the cup: nymphs, other satyrs, even ornamental sphinxes on the sides, transgressing not just the bounds of society but the literal border of the cup.

And violating boundaries is a defining characteristic of humor. Comedy often comes from the flouting of society's rules or expectations, the eruption of scandal, the normal situation turned upside down—a bum becomes rich, a man dresses like a woman, an adult acts like a kid.* Historians say Mesopotamian audiences got major yucks from *The Epic of Gilgamesh*, one of the earliest works of literature (around 2000 BC), when the goddess Ishtar is "mocked as a mortal and behaves like a man." Around 2000 AD, the Norwegian Trickster Loki took over Jim Carrey in *The Mask*, unleashing both his repressed personality and a box office Ishtar (and *Ishtar*) would've killed for.

---

* Do we laugh at drunks because their flailings seem like the clumsy movements of toddlers?

Carrey's fun for everyone, but border-busting isn't always family friendly; it's been said that laughter is a recognition of our undomesticated, primitive selves.

One of Elvis Presley's first TV appearances was on comedian Milton Berle's show in 1956. In this clip, pay special attention to what happens after Elvis slows the song down . . .

See link 3: When the song slows, Elvis gyrates outrageously sexily—the audience laughs nervously and Presley grins.

That stirring in the audience is un-mistakably laced with laughter. Why?

Funny

Presley told no joke. But his very physical presence—his *very* physical presence—was scandalous at the time, his sexuality so overstepping the standard bounds of performance that everyone (including Presley himself) can't help but laugh, out of nervousness and astonishment.*

Tricksters revel in outrageousness and rudeness. The American Indian tribe Winnebago had Wakdjunkaga, who created the world and scattered humanity across the earth with . . . wait for it . . . one enormous fart.

That Joke Is So Old

Whether or not humans were farted into existence, jokes about flatulence have a history that if not glorious, is certainly long.**

---

* The King had a great sense of humor; he bought one of the first VCRs and watched *Monty Python and the Holy Grail* dozens of times.

** For an ~~up-close~~ in-depth examination of this potent topic, see *On Farting* by Valerie Allen. Though please note that this book covers primarily *medieval* farting. (I'm serious.)

The University of Wolverhampton attempted to find the world's oldest recorded joke. The winner dates to 1900 BC and the Sumerians ("Ladies and gentlemen, please welcome 1900 BC and The Sumerians!"):

> *Something which has never occurred since time began; a young woman did not fart in her husband's lap.*

Sex and body functions, always surefire.*

The second oldest, from Ancient Egypt around 1600 BC:

> *How do you entertain a bored pharaoh? Sail a boatload of young women dressed only in fishing nets down the Nile and urge the pharaoh to go catch a fish.*

I didn't say they were good, I said they were old.

A British gag from the tenth century has the distinction of being the oldest joke that's actually funny:

> *What hangs at a man's thigh and wants to poke the hole it's often poked before?*
> *A key.*

As for physical comedy, X-ray analysis of a Paleozoic skeleton discovered in Ethiopia in 2006 revealed faint traces of lemon meringue pie on the skull.

---

* From the *Homeric Hymn to Hermes*, written around 420 BC: "Apollo lifted the child and began to carry him. At this point the infant had a plan. Held aloft in Apollo's hands, he cut loose an omen, an exhausted belly slave, a rude herald of worse to come." Fart *and* shit joke —twofer! (And by the way—next party, try yelling "Who cut the belly slave?")

Okay, that's a lie, but for real, male dancers got laughs by dressing in drag in the ancient Greek cult of Artemis Cordaca, and there's a reference to mooning in Pliny the Elder's *Historia Naturalis*, one of the first published books, from 77 AD.

2

Not In 3-D

MOVIES

Although mooning is timelessly funny (at least if it's Saturday night and you're drunk and in relative proximity to a car window), comedy doesn't always age well. Virgin vampires were no doubt scary to Pliny the Elder (though it was probably Pliny the Younger who bought the books), but humor usually reflects contemporary attitudes and values.

In *Bringing Up Baby* (1938), Cary Grant and Katharine Hepburn are in an expensive restaurant when he accidentally rips her dress; the uproar that ensues comes from the fact that a section of the back of a woman's legs is partly visible. This would be less scandalous for audiences who saw an actress in *Monty Python's Life of Brian* (1979) play an entire scene naked.

As with any art form, film comedy has grown tremendously in sophistication over the years, from the crude antics of the Keystone Kops to the bouncing boobs, jiggling genitalia, and projectile vomit of today.

Okay, it may be more a bell curve than actual growth.

A body part was featured in the first movie ever made, *The Sneeze*, directed by Thomas Edison. Over the course of its three-second running time, you get a powerful sense of what a sneeze was like in 1894. (Word of advice—don't see it in 3-D.)

Exposed Body Part

One of the first figures in American film comedy was Canadian. Vaudevillian Mack Sennett worked for legendary director D. W. Griffith's studio in New Jersey and starred in an early comedy short in 1909. A few years later, he produced the first full-length comedy, *Tillie's Punctured Romance* (1914), with Charlie Chaplin supporting Mabel Normand, who became one of the first woman directors.

Sennett built on European traditions—the comic chase, for instance, was invented by the French. But elegant continental comedians like Max Linder weren't comfortable with the violence and sense of physical abandon that Americans love.

And yet the first American comedy superstar was British. Actually, Charlie Chaplin was the first world superstar. It's difficult today to imagine the dimensions of Chaplin's fame, something rivaled but not exceeded by the Beatles, Elvis, Michael Jackson.

Chaplin's breakthrough was bringing depth to silent comedy through pathos, which came directly from the Victorian sentiment he saw in British music halls (where Stan Laurel was his understudy). His Tramp character—at its core a form of Trickster, the little guy who outwits the big bully—fit into a tradition of British working-class clowns. The difference was that Chaplin took that knockabout tradition and added poetry, sadness, and grace; W.C. Fields called him a "goddam ballet dancer."

Chaplin's output, like Buster Keaton's (chapter 23), was not large. While most comics ground out shorts every few days, Chaplin often needed months, features sometimes taking more than a year. Because there were long periods without new product, at least a dozen comedians filled the void by making imitation Charlie Chaplin movies;

audiences were so desperate that the *fake* Chaplins were hits. There were even Charlies in Japan.

After Chaplin and Keaton, the third great silent clown was Harold Lloyd, whose persona was the go-getting American optimist. Like most comics his character is a fish out of water, but the difference is that Lloyd *puts* himself in those situations, because his persona is aspirational; in *The Freshman* (1925), he launches into a ridiculous dance whenever he meets anyone so they'll remember him.

But despite Lloyd's ingenuity and craftsmanship as a filmmaker, I find his comedies too carefully constructed to pull me in . . . with one exception. *The Kid Brother* (1927) is a terrific movie, beautifully shot and unfailingly clever, and has a bit that I think ranks with any of Keaton or Chaplin.

Harold's a country boy who's met a girl while out walking. They exchange a few words, then she has to go . . .

See link 4: As the girl disappears over a hill, Harold climbs a tree, higher and higher, to say goodbye. Then he loses his balance and crashes to the ground, where his hand lands on a daisy, which he uses for "She loves me, she loves me not . . ."

Babes in the Woods

Despite the achievements of director/actress Mabel Normand and a few others, that scene is typical of women in silent film: they're either the pretty, bland sweetheart or the ugly battle-axe. And though women have made headway in standup and television, even today they're usually second-class citizens in film comedy, cast as bimbos or sluts, or spending their screen time giggling at the zany antics of the male star (a notable recent exception being Kristin Wiig's wonderful performance in *Bridesmaids*).

But the first and biggest exception was Mae West, who rose to fame in the '20s in her play *Sex*, which was not just the foundation but the entire . . . let's see, what's a word that means "something that's built" . . . the entire erection of her career.

In addition to being an iconic personality, West was a wonderful writer, coining among other phrases "A hard man is good to find," "Is that a gun in your pocket or are you just glad to see me?" "When I'm good I'm very good but when I'm bad I'm better," "It's not the men in your life, it's the life in your men," and "I used to be Snow White but I drifted."

The result of her pioneering unabashed attitude? At least partly due to West, the Catholic Church pressured the movie industry to institute the Production Code, a guideline for self-censorship that resulted in thirty years of movies where sophisticated married couples like Nick and Nora Charles in *The Thin Man* slept in separate beds.

Writers Wronged

Women writers like West were rare in early movies but even male scribes were just finding their role; writers barely existed in silent films, which usually consisted of a series of "gags" (comic bits) strung together with a rudimentary plot. Once sound arrived, getting people who could write dialogue became critical and playwrights were imported by the bushel from New York. (When Herman J. Mankiewicz, who later cowrote *Citizen Kane*, moved to Los Angeles, he telegrammed his friend Ben Hecht: "Millions are to be grabbed out here and your only competition is idiots.")

As the years went by, many comedy and even drama directors became defensive about the role of writers, implying a screenplay's just a blueprint or, sometimes, that they and the actors make it up as they go along.

Director Frank Capra had an incredible run of comedy hits in the '30s and '40s, which mysteriously ended when he lost his brilliant writer, Robert Riskin. The story goes that after reading another interview where Capra explained his directorial genius, popularly known as "The Capra Touch," Riskin stormed into Capra's office, threw a hundred blank pieces of paper on his desk and said, "Put the Capra Touch on *that!*"

Around the same time, there were three guys who, though they wrote their own material as they rose through the ranks in vaudeville, ended up using the funniest writers in America to make them funniest team in American film history.

3

Leonard, Adolph, Herbert, and Julius

THE MARX BROTHERS

Leonard was Chico ("Chicko" not "Cheeko"), named after his fondness for women, though his true love was betting; the Marx Brothers' final movies were made mainly to pay off his gambling debts.

Chico could be seen as the Ringo of the group, yet his brothers said that anyone who never learned his lines and showed up only to shoot his scenes then head to the track or a card game and still came off as great as Chico did, was clearly the most talented of them all.

His specialty was wordplay, and he was witty in real life too. When his wife caught him with a chorus girl, Chico claimed he was "just whispering in her mouth."

Adolph was Harpo, who never spoke onscreen. He was by all accounts the sweetest and sanest of the brothers, though "sane" is a relative term here—he was fond of frightening celebrity snoops by playing croquet on his Beverly Hills front lawn in the nude.

While Harpo's technically a mime, he's so different from Marcel Marceau and the other subtle, delicate, evocative mimes of Europe that it's probably safer to say he's noisily mute, relying less on communicating his feelings than honking his taxicab horn, pulling lighted blowtorches from his vest, and chasing any woman in sight.

(For a while, there was also Herbert—Zeppo. Reportedly hysterically funny in real life but consigned to the thankless role of straight man, he left the act and joined a fifth brother, Gummo, to start what became one of the biggest talent agencies in Hollywood.)

And then there's Julius, Groucho, who many people consider the greatest comic of all time, a model for everyone from Woody Allen to Bugs Bunny.

His bent-kneed, loping walk (which, and this is not a joke, has been shown to increase oxygen consumption up to 50 percent), his

Top to bottom: Harpo, Chico, Groucho
Against It

cigar, and the ridiculous grease-paint moustache he brought from vaudeville to Broadway to the movies then grew in real life so people would recognize him—his invented character is funny even before he speaks. And then when he speaks . . .

Here's the newly installed President of Freedonia at the welcoming celebration for the newly installed President of Freedonia . . .

See link 5: Groucho fires off a rapid-fire volley of insults and come-ons to the elegantly clueless Margaret Dumont.

Groucho's nonstop stream-of-consciousness monologues are part of the way he upends social convention, redefining Trickster for the modern age. In the way he snipes at anyone and anything, he updates the brash character of the Yankee (p. 68).

But the unexpected suppleness and lightness—watch him dance— the nonchalant breaking of the fourth wall* by talking to the audience, and the serious delight he takes in unabashed silliness—that is the one and only Groucho.

One of the Original Lines

The Marxes grew up in a Jewish tenement on the Upper East Side of Manhattan and began performing as young kids—first as a music act, gradually becoming comedians, with each boy doing one of the ethnic parodies popular at the time; Chico's ludicrous Italian accent was a remnant of those days. (In *The Coconuts*, Chico spots a disreputable

---

* In plays, actors are often in a room with three walls—the fourth wall is the audience. So the term refers to anything that happens in a form of scripted entertainment that deliberately reminds you you're watching scripted entertainment. The concept goes back to ancient Greece. Aristophanes' *The Birds* (during the making of which no Tippi Hedrens were harmed) was first performed in a competition; at one point, a chorus of birds threatens to crap on the audience if they vote for a different play. There are also examples of less overt "winking" at the audience; after a particularly outrageous plot twist in Shakespeare's *Twelfth Night*, a character says, "If this were play'd upon a stage now, I could condemn it as an improbable fiction."

old associate with a new identity and says, skeptically, "How did you get to be Roscoe W. Chandler?"; the guy answers, "How did you get to be Italian?")

Marx Brothers stage shows were legendary for their energy, goofiness and ad-libs, some of which later appeared in their movies. In the middle of a performance, Groucho suddenly turned to the audience and said urgently, "Is there a doctor in the house?" A man stood up: "I'm a doctor." Groucho: "Howya like the show, doc?"

During another performance, Groucho was doing a scene when Harpo tried to rattle his brother by chasing a chorus girl across the stage, honking his horn. Not missing a beat, Groucho said, "First time I ever saw a taxi hail a passenger."

One night a Marx writer, George S. Kaufman, was talking to a friend at the back of the theater, when he stopped, listened, then said, "Sorry—I thought I heard one of the original lines."

By the time Paramount signed them for pictures, the Marxes were all around forty years old and would be movie stars for less than ten years.

Their first films were essentially photographed stage plays. *Coconuts* was made in 1929, the year sound came to movies, and was shot in Astoria, Queens, during the day while the Marxes performed on Broadway at night in *Animal Crackers*. (At one point in *Coconuts*, Groucho gets his name confused with his character in *Animal Crackers*.)

Later, their movies were written directly for the screen by the best comedy writers around, like Kaufman, S. J. Perelman (p. 61), and Ben Hecht (p. 52), probably the top screenwriter in American history.

The Marx pictures of the early '30s—*Monkey Business, Horse Feathers*, and *Duck Soup*—mark their purely anarchic period. From beginning to end, these films are constantly crazy and practically plotless, their supposed settings (college, ship, mythical kingdom) the thinnest excuses for sketches and songs.

One of the famous bits in *Duck Soup* is the Mirror Routine, which goes back to commedia dell'arte (p. 49), though, as with many comics and many routines, the Marxes made it their own. Harpo and Chico sneak into Groucho's house disguised as Groucho; Groucho hears a noise and hurries downstairs . . .

See link 6: On opposite sides of a nonexistent mirror, Harpo tries to convince Groucho that he's Groucho's reflection.

The Marxes' crazy time ended when they moved from Paramount to MGM in 1934. A meeting was set with legendary MGM studio chief Irving Thalberg, who was late; when he arrived, he found the brothers sitting naked in his office, roasting potatoes in the fireplace. He never kept them waiting again.

Thalberg was convinced they'd be bigger stars with bigger budgets, believable plots and, most importantly, a new sympathetic attitude. They could still be crazy but it had to be in the service of something important; this he defined as helping an insipid young couple in love, which became an integral if unwelcome part of every subsequent Marx Brothers movie.

Thalberg also urged them to try out material for their movies live; they toured the country playing the remaining vaudeville houses, with someone in the audience carefully noting the number and length of each laugh (two seconds is great; four is spectacular). That turned out to be key to the success of their first experiment in quasi-normalcy, *A Night at The Opera*, one of the greatest comedies ever.

Here's one of the funniest bits, known in the comedy community as "The Stateroom Scene." On an ocean liner, Groucho's expecting a romantic visit from Margaret Dumont (his foil in the first *Duck Soup* clip), but he's been put in a tiny cabin with Chico, Harpo, and a friend, and they've just finished ordering a meal consisting primarily of hard-boiled eggs . . .

See link 7: The Marxes negotiate the tiny cabin along with a growing throng of people, including a manicurist who asks if Groucho wants

*his fingernails long or short. Groucho: "Better make 'em short, it's
getting crowded in here."*

Midway through making the follow-up, *A Day at the Races*, Thalberg died, and Groucho always said that's what killed their careers. While there are some classic scenes, the movie's long, drags in the many spots where the Marxes aren't, and includes a horrifying musical number with Harpo and a bunch of black kids.

From Which Direction?

After that it was a slow, steady decline; the Marxes lost interest in the movies and the feeling became mutual. Groucho played supporting roles; his game show *You Bet Your Life* was a modest success on radio then a huge hit on TV, fueled by both scripted and ad-libbed quips. To a tree surgeon: "Tell me, doctor, have you ever fallen out of a patient?" Asked her age, a woman responded, "Let's just say I'm approaching forty." Groucho: "Really? From which direction?"

In 1960 the great director Billy Wilder announced his next movie: *A Day at the United Nations* starring the Marx Brothers, but age and illness killed the project and, in the next few years, Chico and Harpo.

A few years later, the brothers were rediscovered. Groucho toured the country with a one-man show as a new generation saw its own insolence and rebellion in his movies.

But the Marx Brothers represent something more primal than a particular generation; in fact, each of the Marxes can be seen as a different aspect of Trickster . . .

Wordplay? When Groucho presents a contract with a standard sanity clause, Chico scoffs, "You can't fool me—there ain't no Sanity Claus."

Exaggerated sexuality? Harpo's libido was so off the charts that it seemed to daze and confuse the censors of the time. In *Duck Soup*, he gallops through a town on horseback, sees a girl in a window, and rides into her house and her bedroom. Later, at the foot of the bed, we see his shoes, her shoes, and a pair of horseshoes, then Harpo in bed . . . with the horse.

Insulting any and everyone? Groucho leaving a party (in real life), to host: "I've had a wonderful evening. Unfortunately, this wasn't it."

Still, the Marx Brothers were less archetypal than American to the core. While there have been comics called "the Chaplin of Mexico" and "the Keaton of France," there's never been a Marx Brothers of anywhere. It's hard to find their commitment to chaos in any other society's popular art; it's pretty much impossible to imagine them in a different culture.

In the way no one and nothing is safe when they're around, I think of Marlon Brando in *The Wild One* when he's asked what he's rebelling against and answers, "Whaddya got?" The Marx version, sung by Groucho in *Horse Feathers*: "Whatever it is, I'm against it."

In a way, they're even more anarchic than Trickster, whose tales were often used to teach lessons. The Marx Brothers never tried to teach anything or, in their best movies, help anyone, even themselves. They only wanted to chase women, play music, and destroy stuff— stuff like wealth, power, arrogance, pomposity . . . ultimately even order, society.

Maybe they *are* teaching a lesson: that it's possible to rebel against, or just ignore, society's restraints; that human beings have the power to let go and be free.

4

More History of Ha!

THE ANCIENT WORLD

In his later years, Groucho ran into an odd phenomenon: people who wanted him to insult them. After all, being ridiculed by Groucho Marx was a mark of distinction—he didn't just insult anybody. (Actually, he did.) Even the rich and powerful found Groucho's insults "delightful," which, he suspected, was a way of diminishing the criticism.

It's counterintuitive, but people in power have long been fond of employing someone to mock them, maybe because it's better to "keep your enemies closer." It all started during Egypt's Fifth Dynasty, around 2400 BC, when a foreign slave was brought to serve at the pharoah's palace. Not knowing proper court behavior, the slave's bumbling antics were deemed high-larious, and he was allowed to say irreverent and insulting things about the court, the gods, even the pharaoh.

Thus was created the Court Jester, whose role is shown by the joker in a deck of cards (invented in ninth-century China): the joker isn't in the royal family or a member of any suit, he's not even really part of the pack, yet he's potentially the most powerful card in the deck. His costume—the "motley"—is a patchwork of different colors and shapes, mocking the regular lines and colors we usually wear, symbolizing the way comedy disrupts and reconfigures conventional society's strictures. The jester/joker, like the comedian, is outside society and obeys no rules—he is literally "wild." *

The influence of jesters on their masters has been referenced countless times, not least by Shakespeare in *King Lear*, whose jester is a man who knows the truth but disguises it with jokes.

But a real-life example comes from ancient China. The Emperor

Herm, Pre-Circumcision

Shih Huang-ti ordered construction of a Wall that, as Richard Nixon later noted, was really Great. After it was built, Huang-ti ordered it painted. His advisors feared that would bankrupt the empire but he ignored them; then his jester made fun of the idea and the Emperor changed his mind.

Which explains the ancient Chinese scroll reading "Now what're we gonna do with two million gallons of primer?"

Greece Is the Word, or: Acropolis Now

Ancient Greece's Trickster was Hermes, a messenger who travelled between the gods and humanity. He was so important to Greek civilization that the statues marking the boundaries of each landowner's property were called *herms*. Since

---

* In the Middle Ages, jesters were frequently hunchbacks or dwarves—other forms of "outsiders."

there were thousands, no one worried about making herms recognizable; most were just pillars with a head shape . . . and a giant erect penis. (Presumably a more direct way of indicating gender than a top hat.)

In Athens one night someone, probably a drunk, knocked all the penises off the herms, and since they were cultural symbols as much as property markers, it was considered a significant crime. When the great General Alcibiades was accused he went into exile, and some blame the failure of the Peloponnesian Expedition on his absence. So perhaps the greatest civilization in history lost a war due to wacky hijinks.

Hermes gave his name to a field of linguistics: *hermeneutics*, the study of alternate interpretations of communication—reading between the lines, revealing meanings that aren't obvious, which is the role of Trickster. And the comedian.

So what's the connection between Greek-statue penis-breaking and Zach Galifianakas? It's the comedian as boundary marker. While herms monitored society's physical borders, Tricksters and comics play a metaphorical role, policing moral boundaries. They represent aspects of the anarchy we all fear but secretly crave—unrestrained sexuality, turning society upside down, and unrestrained sexuality.

And speaking of comedians . . .

5

Live from Giggles

STANDUP

Hey, it's great to be in [YOUR TOWN]. Anyone here from [YOUR STATE] tonight? Beautiful! I'm from California myself. Hey, Californians are crazy, aren't they? The state's bankrupt, the governor was a weightlifter and the only thing to take your mind off the earthquakes are the wildfires. Still, it's a beautiful place—the mountains, the canyons, the rivers, the grass . . . But enough about medical marijuana.

What a gorgeous book this is, huh? Love that lining. Yeah, go ahead, rub it. Faster. Faster!

Okay, gimme a minute.

For those of you using e-readers, rub the screen. Don't worry, I won't byte.

Get it?!!!

Well, I see by the ole sundial my time's just about up so . . . TV commercials! I love TV commercials, and speaking of bad cooking my ex-wife's so fat you should see the alimony I'm paying and doctors, y'know what I'm saying? And airplane travel and traffic and those little packets of ketchup and dogs, no, really, dogs! You been beautiful, don't forget to tip your waitress, here's a good tip, don't wait tables in a book, I love you all, g'night!

Only Enough to Win

Standup comedy is like anything else—there's hack and there's class and 'twas ever thus. I guarantee there was some guy in the Old West saying, "How 'bout those nutty wagon trains? And don't get me started on Indian attacks . . ."

American standup began with people like Mark Twain and, oddly enough, Oscar Wilde—charismatic speakers who travelled the country giving lectures filled with witticisms and social commentary.

The "monologists" in music halls and vaudeville did the same thing, but people like Twain and Wilde had an advantage because in comedy, personality is everything—the beginning of this chapter is generic less because of its content than in the way it's presented. Successful standups have well-honed personas that make the jokes funnier by making them seem personal.

In vaudeville, persona was less personal than cultural, as comics attempted to pre-sell their jokes through ethnicity, usually using racial stereotypes—as we've seen, the Marx Brothers began that way. Modern standup began when comics started getting laughs by using themselves instead of ethnicity, and one of the first to do that was Bob Hope.

Un-American

Love him or hate him, Hope is the iconic American standup, the only flaw with that characterization being that Leslie Townes Hope was born in London in 1903. But he lived to one hundred, and you can trace the evolution of twentieth-century American entertainment through his career. To get a sense of its scope, he first appeared on television before there *was* television, on a test broadcast in 1932.

When he started doing TV for real in the '50s, he more or less ruled the ratings for forty years.

But while he was a hit on radio, TV, and in the movies, the heart of Hope was standup, travelling the world accompanied by one golf club and dozens of writers, including those at home who were on call for jokes 24/365, among them Larry Gelbart (Sid Caesar, *Tootsie*, TV's *M*A*S*H*) and Woody Allen (chapter 13).

Like Jack Benny, Hope started as a fast-talking, smart-aleck braggart, an offshoot of the Yankee prototype (p. 68), but he found his persona as a guy who was on the prowl for women but shy when he got them; pushy, but a coward when pushed; always the odd man out.

One of my favorite Hope gags is in a movie where he's a cowboy wannabe in the Old West. Trying to impress some tough guys in a saloon, he swaggers around in gigantic chaps and clanking spurs, slams his fist on the bar and says, "Gimme a milk." When the cowboys look unimpressed he snarls, "In a dirty glass."

Hope's friend Milton Berle was notorious in the comedy world for two things: that he stole any joke within earshot (he was semi-affectionately called "The Thief of Bad Gags") and that he was reputed to have the largest penis in show business. At New York's show-biz hangout the Friars Club, Berle was going to the bathroom and another comic challenged him to compare penises. "Okay," said Berle, "but I'm only gonna take out enough to win."

Comedy Jazz

Hope and Berle were in their prime in the '50s but the world was changing, and young people lost interest in standups delivering a series of barely related one-liners. The Beat Generation, with its skewed, "outsider" view of the world, made itself felt everywhere, even in comedy, where the incredibly strange, often inspired poet and monologist Lord Buckley gained Beat cred as the first "jazz comedian." His most famous routine, "The Nazz," is Buckley's be-bop version of Jesus healing the lame . . .

See link 8: Lord Buckley tells how "The Nazz look at the little cat with the bent frame and he put the Golden Eyes of Love on this here little kittie . . ."

Buckley was a trip but ultimately a cult figure. Mort Sahl, while arguably of the hipster counterculture as well, broke through to the mainstream with an aggressively political act.

A fierce critic of the conservatives then in power (in the '60s he became an equally fierce critic of liberals), Sahl put out the first live comedy album in 1958 and was the first standup to make the cover of *Time*. Unlike traditional nightclub comics, he wrote his own material; in fact, he often improvised it onstage while looking through the day's newspaper. (Today he'd surf Yahoo! News with his iPhone.)

Sahl came to prominence at the perfect time for political humor, as Senator Joe McCarthy and his Senate subcommittee persecuted thousands for supposed Communist sympathies. Sahl tore into the McCarthyites like a vulture into carrion: "Every time Russia throws an American in jail, the Un-American Activities Committee retaliates by throwing an American in jail."

But beyond politics, his humor captured the spirit of the times. "Guy walks into a hotel and goes to the desk clerk, a college kid working nights. The guy hands the clerk a note: 'Give me all the money. Act normal.' Kid writes back, 'Define normal.'"

Another comic trod some of the same territory, took even bigger risks, and paid the price. The history of standup comedy divides pretty clearly into pre- and post–Lenny Bruce.

Not a Comedian

Lenny's mother was a stripper, and he grew up in seedy clubs, so blunt talk came naturally to him. (If you're interested in Bruce's life and don't want to read a book, get the Dustin Hoffman movie *Lenny*.)

The mother-in-law jokes that still dominated nightclub comedy seemed antediluvian when Lenny talked about sex ("A man will fuck mud," he noted); drugs (he was a hopeless heroin addict); and especially religion (maybe his most famous routine was about ad-men selling religions as products). As for his own beliefs, he was Jewish, secular . . . and pugnacious.

> *A lot of people say to me, "Why did you kill Christ?" I dunno . . . It was one of those parties, got out of hand, you know. We killed him because he didn't want to become a doctor.*

He had a routine that started "Any niggers here tonight?" then went through every ethnic slur, ending by saying, "It's the suppression of the word that gives it the power."*

This led to Richard Pryor's adoption of "nigger" as an expression of racial pride (p. 42), while Lenny's unselfconscious obscenities opened the door for George Carlin's "Seven Words You Can't Say on Television" routine, which needed the Supreme Court to keep it off the air. But as Lenny said, "Take away the right to say 'fuck' and you take away the right to say 'fuck the government.'"

Even his nonpolitical stuff was charged. A prison warden talks to convicts during a riot: "We're giving in to your demands, men. Except for the vibrators."

In one bit, he describes Christ and Moses showing up at St. Patrick's Cathedral . . .

See link 9: Lenny's famously heretical routine where Cardinal Spellman and Bishop Sheen are irritated when Christ and Moses appear at a service.

---

* And there are lots of powerful words out there: Wikipedia—which I never look at and provided none of the information in this book, you don't even have to check—lists twenty-one pages of racial slurs, from "Abie" (turn-of-the-twentieth-century American Jews) to "Zipperhead" (North Koreans during the Korean War).

Especially at the end of his career, when he read from transcripts of his latest obscenity trial, Lenny wasn't always a rib-tickler. He'd say, "I'm sorry I haven't been funny. I'm not a comedian. I'm Lenny Bruce."

The hostility of Hope and the comedy establishment to the success of Sahl, along with the relentless persecution of Lenny Bruce, inspired traditional comics like Carlin and Pryor to dump their middlebrow routines and embrace sex, drugs, and rock 'n' roll. Carlin said, "I find out where they draw the line then step across it."

Women Aren't Funny

Women are underrepresented in standup but only because they're not funny. One reason is that they're uncomfortable with verbal aggression, body functions, sex, and violence—the four basic food groups of comedy. Yes, there are exceptions—Lucy then, Tina now—but everyone knows real women don't get laughs.

Of course, they're great for laughing *at*: harpy mothers-in-law, dumb blondes, bad drivers, frigid virgins, castrating sexpots, nagging wives. But women *being* funny? I don't think so.

Okay, I do. But the above was taken as gospel in the past and is still believed by a lot of the guys who dominate professional comedy today.

One of the first female comics was Phyllis Diller, who's very funny but tough to watch now—her humor was self-misogynistic, insulting her looks: "I'm the only woman who can walk through Central Park at night and reduce the crime rate."

Another pioneer was Joan Rivers, who started out with Woody Allen in Greenwich Village, a leotard-wearing Barnard intellectual. That changed.

When Roseanne Barr arrived in the late '80s, she represented a seismic shift—a plain, overweight, confident working-class woman who stood up for herself and her rights, and was really funny.

The women who break through bring a radically different perspective to standup. Rita Rudner: "One of my friends told me she was in labor for thirty-six hours. I don't even want to do anything that feels *good* for thirty-six hours." More recently, edgy female comics have pushed into previously unthinkable territory. Amy Schumer: "I just slept with my high school crush. But now he expects me to go to his graduation. [Beat.] Like I know where I'm gonna be in three years." Sarah Silverman: "I was raped by a doctor. Which is so bittersweet for a Jewish girl."

Black People Are Scary

Like women, blacks were long marginalized in the comedy world, but at least they had their own clubs: the "Chitlin' Circuit," where Moms Mabley—spiritual mother of Whoopie Goldberg—traded electrifyingly obscene one-liners with her almost entirely male counterparts, guys like Redd Foxx. A few black performers like Dick Gregory and Godfrey Cambridge also appealed to white audiences, yet flirted dangerously with political and racial humor.

Cambridge had a joke that began with a "colored fellow" looking up at the sky . . .

See link 10: God tells the guy that the reason he has black skin, "nappy" hair, and long legs to help him survive in the jungle. Guy: "So what the hell am I doing in Cleveland?"

Bill Cosby was the most popular comic, black or white, of the '60s. His routines transcended race by talking about kids and parenting—Steve Martin says he was one of the first comics to tell jokes you could actually believe were true.

Cosby's act may have been racially neutral, but he was always aware of race, especially when he joined white actor Robert Culp in the TV series *I Spy.* There were boycotts by Southern TV stations, but Cosby defused the tension with his humor and charm. This was at a time when there was a huge uproar when the white William Shatner embraced the black Nichelle Nichols on an episode of *Star Trek*, even though the plot had them forced to kiss by evil aliens.

And then along came Richard.

6

"That Nigger's Crazy!"

RICHARD PRYOR

Richard Pryor was a mass of contradictions—black power advocate, humanist; self-aware, self-destructive; egotistical, insecure.

His explorations of race—and most importantly, himself—put him in a category separate from the other black comics he's usually grouped with and who have openly idolized him—people like Dave Chapelle, Chris Rock, and Eddie Murphy, who took the cockiness from Pryor's political phase but missed the vulnerability he had even then.

Pryor's mother was a prostitute, and he grew up in a whorehouse run by his grandmother, who often beat him. On the plus side, it's always nice to have a family business.

As a teen he was in the Army for two years but spent almost the whole time in jail for beating up a white soldier who was enjoying a racist movie. Discharged at nineteen, he worked for a Mafia-owned club. When

Pixilated

a stripper had trouble getting paid, Pryor was so mad he got a cap pistol and threatened to rob the owner, who didn't have him killed because he thought it was so funny.

Genital Pixilation

Inspired by Cosby, Pryor started as a straightforward, non-racial, inoffensive comic. He got enormously popular then one night in 1969, he went onstage in Vegas; looked out at the rich, white crowd; said, "What the fuck am I doing here?" and walked off, in what was probably part disgust at what he saw as the softness of his act and part nervous breakdown. (A year later, it was Carlin's turn—he changed his act after getting fired by a Vegas hotel for "saying 'shit' in a town where the big game is craps.")

Pryor dropped out of the business and became radicalized, listening to Marvin Gaye, hanging in Berkeley with Huey Newton, reading *The Autobiography of Malcolm X*. When he returned to standup, he was as much social commentator as comic. His act became more like he talked, with lots of profanity, especially the word "nigger."

As Lenny Bruce had urged (p. 37), Pryor was determined to strip the word of its power by reclaiming it from both white racists and Black Power activists, who used it to describe blacks who wouldn't join an armed revolution. Dick Gregory, another black activist comic, made it the title of his autobiography, with a dedication to his mother: "If you ever hear the word again, remember they're advertising my book."

For Pryor, "niggers" were the hustlers, whores, junkies, and winos of his childhood, people who were an embarrassment to both whites and blacks. By bringing his audiences into their world, by making the despised human, he elevated both them and the audience.

It was new territory and there was really no place for it. Pryor got a TV variety series in 1977, but he couldn't take the censorship and quit after four episodes, the last of which he opened standing onstage naked with his genitals pixilated. (And if you've ever had your genitals pixilated, you know how painful that can be.)

He visited Africa in 1979 and described hearing a voice inside him say, "Do you see any niggers here?" He didn't and decided never to use the word again. (Evidently the voice didn't say anything about "motherfucker.")

After bringing Black Power sensibility to standup, by the end of his career Pryor became, like Malcolm X, more open and accepting of the possibility of racial harmony. And after seeing how it was thrown around in rap and hip-hop, he condemned *anyone* using the N-word.

But of all his trailblazing achievements, none topped the way in which, with humor and courage, Pryor used the most painful parts of own life for his act: his horrible childhood, his heart attack, his drug addiction. In 1980 he set himself on fire while freebasing cocaine; in his act, he'd light a match, move it left to right and say, "What's this? Richard Pryor running down the street." Bill Cosby: "For Richard, the line between comedy and tragedy is as fine as you can paint it."

Probably the greatest standup show ever filmed was 1978's *Richard Pryor Live in Concert . . .*

See link 11: Pryor becomes his own heart as it tries to kill him.

He talked honestly about racism; Damon Wayans said Pryor was the first black man to make fun of white people onstage . . . and live. And when he dealt with sex it was not only honest but self-lacerating, as he looked at what women need from men and vice versa, laying open his own insecurities and failings.

Director Barnet Kellman talks about comedy as sacrifice; the comedian makes a fool of himself, giving up his dignity and privacy to make us realize we all have the same problems. Comic D. L. Hughley: "All of us spend our lives hoping nobody finds out what we're afraid of. Richard spent his life *showing* people what he was afraid of."

Pryor's drug addiction and erratic behavior meant that his career was essentially over by his mid-forties; he later got multiple sclerosis and died at fifty-five.

In 1998 Pryor was given the first Kennedy Center Mark Twain Prize for American Humor, the citation reading: "He forced us to look at large social questions of race and the more tragicomic aspects of the human condition, projecting, like Twain, a generosity of spirit that unites us."

In a 2004 Comedy Central poll, he was voted the greatest standup of all time.

7

Even More History of Ha!

ARISTOTLE TO RESTORATION

So, where did we leave the Greeks? Okay, reverse search—Greeks herms Trickster unrestrained sexuality. Cool.

Humor in ancient Greece was more than mythology and metaphors; it's there that funny went long-form with the first theatrical comedies.

It was the Greeks who said the difference between comedy and tragedy is the ending—happy comedy, sad tragedy; comedy wedding, tragedy funeral. (The movie *Four Weddings and a Funeral* would be intensely confusing to them.) Of course, you could say a wedding and marriage don't necessarily mean a happy ending, but let's keep your personal life out of this.

Theater grew out of religious festivals in ancient Egypt, but it was formalized in Greece. The first plays, all tragedies, were performed in the late sixth century BC—comedies didn't appear till a hundred years later.

The professionalization of humor faced significant obstacles in two guys named Plato and Aristotle; both thought laughter was a malicious reaction to the ignorance of others. Because moral people having such a hateful response could upset the social order, Plato

Anti-Giggle

actually forbid leaders of his imaginary city-state, the Republic, to laugh.*

Aristotle was looser—he felt humor could show people how to lead better lives and wrote a book about comedy that is lost to history, though the surviving part, *Poetics*, is the first codification of the rules of drama.

Poetics says that comedy began with the *komos*, a fertility ritual in which a group of men sang and danced around a giant phallus. This gives new meaning to the term "standup."**

The 2300 Year Old Virgin

Aristotle saw comedy as a low art form because it dealt with low people like peasants and slaves, doing immoral or ridiculous things. For Aristotle, a typical comedy had a hapless, ugly guy who can't do anything right eventually getting what he wants, usually a pretty girl. Clearly Aristotle was looking to collaborate with Judd Apatow.

---

* The idea of laughter as sinister persisted for thousands of years. In the eighteenth century, Lord Chesterfield wrote, "There is nothing so illiberal, and so ill-bred, as audible laughter," and it's been described with varying derision as "the mind sneezing" (Wyndham Lewis), "the hiccup of a fool" (John Ray), the mark of "a vacant mind" (Oliver Goldsmith), and "a kind of sickness—vulgar, invariably injurious and sometimes fatal." (George Vasey). Even today there are prohibitions: a fatwa issued in Saudi Arabia forbids women to write "LOL" in online posts, because the thought of a woman laughing would send men into a sexual frenzy. Frankly, I'm getting excited right now, and it was me who wrote it.

** And the tradition continues. In Kawasaki, Japan, a Shinto harvest festival called the *Kanamara Matsuri* (a name evidently preferred to Penispalooza) features a gala penis parade, yummy penis pops, penis rides for the kiddies, and in a classy nod to gender equity, matching penis and vagina cakes.

In Athens, you could see political satire performed by comic poets and in the plays of Aristophanes, who worked blue, with lots of sex and scatology.

Gradually, stock comic characters emerged, like *senex iratus*—the grumpy old man who tries to stop his kid from getting married and ends up doing the same things he got mad at the kid for, which makes ancient Greek theater at its pinnacle roughly equivalent to an ABC sitcom of the '80s.

Roman Follies

While the Greeks explored Good, Evil, and the meaning of life, the Romans had drunk guys falling down.

They liked their comedy gross, full of dancing, booze, greed, obscenity, and dumb jokes. Because of the crudeness on stage, while actors were respected in Greece, in Rome they were seen as inferior. (And this from a culture that used human urine as mouthwash.)

Roman humor could be rough. Pliny the Elder reported that the sixth century BC poet Hipponax wrote satires so cruel that their subjects hanged themselves.* Fear of prosecution for libel was an issue even then, but another Roman satirist, Horace, was confident that the quality of his poems would protect him: "Should Caesar think my verses smart / a laugh will cut the matter short / the case will fall apart / and defendant leaves the court." (That poem became a legal adage, still used today: *solventur risu tabulae*—essentially, "The case is laughed out of court."

The Romans' take on Trickster was false kings. During the festival of Saturnalia, a Lord of Misrule was chosen and could turn any law on its head, like forcing masters to wait on their slaves.

---

* In early Germanic and Celtic societies, targets of satirical songs were said to break out in boils, commit suicide, and sometimes drop dead of shame.

In medieval Europe this became the Feast of Fools, a near-orgy of costumes, drinking, dancing, and rowdy revelry—damn, where's the Time Machine when you need it?—where the clergy was mocked and a young boy declared bishop.

Today, at Mardi Gras in New Orleans, false kings rule (get it?!) as parades feature hundreds of mock monarchs. The difference is that in some ancient celebrations the fakers had real authority, if only for a short time. But if society gave someone the power to turn everything upside down, a price had to be paid. At the end of Saturnalia, the false king was killed; after Mardi Gras, three hundred thousand people have hangovers.

Middle-Age Spread

The Middle Ages saw the appearance of European "jest-books," which included snipes and japes (incidentally, the name of my law firm) about stupid peasants, petty and amorous priests, and stupid, petty, amorous, talkative, and debauched women. "Take my chattel, please!"

Also hanging around Europe were the Goliards, a loose-knit group of insurgent clerical students who mocked the Church in satirical verse. Their antics, denounced as "scurrilous" from the pulpit, included "wanton songs," dressing up donkeys, eating pudding on the altar, and pulling herring along the ground. Par-tay!

Goliard poems also bragged about their fighting, drinking, gambling, and sexual exploits, indicating that the roots of rap go further back than is usually thought.

Lacking TV and YouTube, the Middle Ages even saw a subgenre of humorous art. In Holland, Jan Steen's portraits of domestic pandemonium and salacious couplings would have scandalized the Burgermeisters (or, as we know them, Burger Kings) except that they always had a moralizing tone, which reminds me of the Python sketch where a new professor's told he's welcome to teach any of great socialist thinkers as long as he makes it clear they're wrong.

In Ming Dynasty China, "cross-talk" performers used rapid-fire dialogue filled with puns—probably the closest Western equivalent is "Who's on First" (p. 71). Five hundred years later, after the Cultural Revolution, when the infamous Gang of Four was arrested, it was cross-talk performers who made the first public denunciations.

Punch, Meet Judy

The Renaissance is, of course, known for its remarkable outpouring of creativity in comedy. I understand there were also some painters then, but screw that; for our purposes, the Renaissance means *commedia dell'arte*—"comedy of art," an improvisational form that began in the fifteenth century and is still around today.

Travelling troupes of masked actors performed outside with a few props, such as a club made of two wooden slats used for hitting people: the *battocchio* or, in English, "slap stick."

One commedia character was a Trickster named Pulcinella who, a few hundred years later, would costar in British Punch and Judy puppet shows. By then, in Elizabethan England, theatrical comedy focused mainly on characters with one overriding trait or "humour." (From ancient Greece to the mid nineteenth century, Western medicine was based on the treatment of humours, which, unfortunately, turned out not to exist.)

English playwrights like Ben Jonson revived the Greek tradition of stock characters, which later combined with the Comedy of Manners to become Restoration Comedy, brimming with satire and sex. This was encouraged by Charles II, who, with seven mistresses and twelve children, clearly understood satire, not to mention sex.

And speaking of sex . . .

8

Theatuh

THE FRONT PAGE

There isn't really much sex in this chapter. But be honest, would you have kept reading if I said "Speaking of theater"? (Readers born after 2000 can best understand theater as live Pay YouTube.)

In a nation founded by pilgrims, the entertainment industry had some trouble getting started—most of the New England colonies banned "painted vanities." Professional actors and theaters first appeared in the eighteenth century, although it was said then that actors were of low morals and actresses had no virtue, beliefs considered laughable today.

Within a hundred years, theater had become big business—actors would find a money-making property and tour with it for years, audiences coming to see the same production again and again: essentially, live-action reruns. And since there was no copyright, anyone could do anything; in the 1890s, there were more than five hundred separate productions of *Uncle Tom's Cabin*.*

Sadly, theatrical comedy was an unindicted co-conspirator in the murder of our greatest president.

---

* Ninety years later, Eugene O'Neill's *Long Day's Journey into Night* featured a father who destroyed his family by touring the country for decades in a low-rent production of *The Count of Monte Cristo*.

Timing

John Wilkes Booth was a member of the most distinguished theater family in America; his brother Edwin was the nation's foremost Shakespearean actor. On April 14, 1865, John Wilkes—a Confederate sympathizer—used his fame to get into Abraham Lincoln's box during a performance of the comedy *Our American Cousin.*

Knowing the play well, Booth waited till a character said, "Don't know the manners of good society, eh? Well, I guess I know enough to turn *you* inside out, you sockdologizing old man-trap." He then fired, hoping the gunshot would be masked by the audience's helpless howling at "sockdologizing old man-trap," a surefire laugh line if ever I heard one.

A Cross Between a Bootlegger and a Whore

The first hit stage comedy that can properly be called modern was a product of the Roaring Twenties.

Ben Hecht has come up already; though not well known today, this was one amazing guy. A child prodigy—concert violinist at ten, circus acrobat at twelve—he was working as a reporter in Chicago when he got that telegram from Herman J. Mankiewicz (p. 18) and moved West, where he became "the Shakespeare of Hollywood," winning the first Oscar for Best Screenplay and writing more than seventy films and thirty-five books, including Marilyn Monroe's autobiography.*

Marilyn Monroe

The most formative experience of Hecht's life was working for a Chicago newspaper. His bestselling autobiography, *Child of the Century*, has great stories about his adventures; in fact, *his* story was made into a 1969 movie called *Gaily, Gaily*.

But the best way to learn about those days is from a play he wrote with fellow reporter Charles MacArthur.

The Front Page brings an amazing array of characters from '20s Chicago onto the stage—bitter prostitutes, amoral thugs, politicians on the take, moronic functionaries, confused political radicals, corrupt cops—all drawn without the slightest sentimentality.

Hecht and MacArthur's most cynical portrait, maybe the most insulting and scabrous libel of a profession in history, is of newspaper reporters, who are shown as lazy, venal, lying, conniving, racist,

---

* Hecht was also an activist for civil rights and Zionist causes; he wrote a play to raise funds to buy a ship, later named the S.S. Ben Hecht, which brought Holocaust survivors to America—one of the actors was a young Marlon Brando.

misogynist, and misanthropic: "a cross," one character says, "between a bootlegger and a whore."

Comedy Sex Change

The play is set in the grim and grubby Press Room of the Chicago Criminal Courts Building, where reporters pass the time with poker and wisecracks while awaiting the execution of a radical for murder. But Hildy Johnson wants out; he's going to marry a society girl whose father will set him up in business and get him away from newspapers and Chicago.

Hildy's devious boss Walter Burns will do anything to stop his star reporter from leaving, including sabotaging his marriage. When the radical escapes from jail and staggers into the Press Room, Hildy—the only one there—crams him into a rolltop desk, calls Walter, and they spend the rest of the play scheming to get the desk out of a building crawling with reporters and cops.

If it sounds sensational, it is. Act 1 ends with the stage riddled with bullets; Act 2 ends with Hildy stuffing the radical in the desk while Burns works the phones to pull everything else off the front page. And the finale has one of the most famous curtain lines in theater history: "The son-of-a-bitch stole my watch!," the context of which I'll leave you to discover for yourself.

As directed on Broadway by George S. Kaufman, *The Front Page* was like a stink bomb exploding in a library; there'd never been such a raucous, raunchy, riot of a play. It was the hit of all hits, becoming a movie that was remade nine times; one was the classic screwball comedy *His Girl Friday*, where Hecht, MacArthur, and director Howard Hawks gave Hildy a sex change into Rosalind Russell. It was also done by Billy Wilder with Jack Lemmon and Walter Matthau, and turned into four TV shows and a British musical.

A famous bit from *His Girl Friday* gives an idea of the play's pace and drive. With the murderer in the desk, Burns (Cary Grant) remakes the paper's front page while Hildy (Russell) pounds out the story as her fiancé tries to get her on a train out of town . . .

See link 12: With blistering dialogue, Burns barks out orders on the phone as Hildy types the story while fending off her fiancé.

I think America's love for such a tough, cynical play says something about how we see ourselves. The idealistic radical tells his hooker friend, "Humanity is a wonderful thing." She says, "No it ain't."

For all our moral posturing, many Americans are willing to go beyond purple mountains and fruity plains to revel in a land filled with scurrilous characters, violence, blasphemy, passion, and a take-no-prisoners desperation for success—in other words, a country with energy, excitement, and life.

And where there's life, there's death . . .

9

Nights of the Round Table

PROSE

Dorothy Parker, perhaps the darkest of all American funny people, wrote a poem listing the downsides of various methods of committing suicide, wanly concluding, "You might as well live." Her vicious social circle, the Algonquin Round Table—a weekly gathering of wits at Manhattan's Algonquin Hotel during the '20s—became legendary for the quotes it generated, many by Parker.

In a game, she was challenged to use word *horticulture* in a sentence and said, "You can lead a horticulture but you can't make her think." She referred to a woman who "speaks eighteen languages and can't say no in any of them."

Her reviews could be devastating. She wrote of a novel that was "not to be tossed aside but to be hurled with great force," and said of Katharine Hepburn in a play, "She runs the gamut of emotions from A to B." And she didn't spare herself: at a party, she warned, "One more drink and I'll be under the host."

The Grand Leap of the Whale

It's doubtful that Parker considered herself a direct descendent of Benjamin Franklin, but at least in the field of humorous prose, she was. (Readers born after 2000 can best understand prose as a blog viewed on wireless papyrus.) Franklin may not have been the first funny writer in America but he was the first to discover electricity. And not to belittle our beloved Founding Father in any way, but if

Whale Watcher

he'd had the foresight to invent the light bulb he wouldn't have had to invent bifocals.

Along with most early American humorists, Franklin's *bon mots* may seem less *bon* to us than to his original audiences; his topical references are now historical and comedic styles have changed. But even today, some of Franklin's stuff is surprisingly sharp.

In 1765 he wrote, "Englishmen are apt to be silent when they have nothing to say; to be sullen when they are silent; and, when they are silent, to hang themselves."

And this kind of sounds like an eighteenth-century Letterman monologue:

> *An account in the papers last week said the inhabitants of Canada are making preparations for a cod and whale fishery in the Upper Lakes. Ignorant people may object that the Upper Lakes are salt water. But let them know that the grand leap of the whale in that chase up the falls of Niagara is esteemed, by all who have seen it, as one of the finest spectacles in nature.*

But most eighteenth- and nineteenth-century comic prose consists of difficult-to-read and not particularly funny dialect stories. Mark Twain—or as he was known to his bill collectors, Samuel Clemens—is a different matter. Many people, including your eighth-grade English teacher, consider *Huckleberry Finn* the Great

American Novel, and with the exception of the disastrous ending, I probably agree.

Polyp Porn

Finn was published in 1884; for the next forty-six years, no one in America wrote, or even did, anything funny.

Then one evening, Algonquin regular Robert Benchley left a restaurant with his grandson Peter (who grew up to write the novel *Jaws*). Seeing a uniformed man at the door, Benchley asked, "Would you get us a taxi?" The man was stone-faced. "I happen to be an admiral in the United States Navy." "All right then," said Benchley, "get us a battleship."

Robert Benchley was the patron saint of American absurdity. Writer, critic, and to his own amazement, Hollywood movie star, Benchley is a touchstone for the most fundamental of American freedoms: the right to be silly.

Benchley began (like most of the writers on *The Simpsons*) at the *Harvard Lampoon*. He was doing columns for *The New Yorker* when his Algonquin pals decided to put on a show. His monologue "The Treasurer's Report" became so popular that it was shot as one of the first sound films. Those with a taste for the salacious, however, may prefer his second short; like so many writers corrupted by Hollywood, Benchley took a perfectly decent essay—"The Social Life of the Newt"—and turned it into the scandalous "Sex Life of the Polyp" . . .

Awake

See link 13: Benchley delicately discusses the mating habits of a creature with no definitive gender.

After the success of these shorts, Benchley spent time in Hollywood for the rest of his life, winning an Oscar for "How to Sleep" and appearing as the star's genial best friend in dozens of movies. He kept writing for the *New Yorker* and published collections of his columns—six hundred in twelve volumes.

Despite titles like "Future Man: Tree or Mammal," "Uncle Edith's Ghost Story," and "Dog Libel," Benchley's pieces were usually wry musings on ordinary events. But when he strays from Seinfeld-style observational humor into pure flights of fancy, he's brilliant. Here's an excerpt from "The Rope Trick Explained":

> *While in India, a friend of mine, a Mr. MacGregor, assisted me in confusing the natives, in more ways than one. We dressed up in Indian costume, for one thing. This confused even us but we took it good-naturedly.*
>
> *Then I announced to a group of natives, who were standing open-mouthed (ready to bite us, possibly), that Mr. MacGregor and I would perform the famous Indian Rope Trick under their very noses. This was like stealing thunder from a child.*
>
> *Stationing myself at the foot of a rope which extended upward into the air with no apparent support at the other end, I suggested to Mr. MacGregor that he climb it. "Who—me?" he asked, hitching his tunic around his torso.*
>
> *This took up some time, during which part of our audience left ... [Then] Mr. MacGregor laid hands on the rope and, in a trice, was at its top. It wasn't a very good trice, especially when viewed from below, but it served to bring a gasp of astonishment from the little group, many of whom walked away ...*
>
> *"Are there any questions?" I asked the mob. "What is Clark Gable like?" someone said. "He's a very nice fellow," I answered. "Modest and unassuming. I see quite a lot of him when I am in Hollywood."*
>
> *There was a scramble for my autograph at this, and the party moved on, insisting that I go with them for a drink and tell them more about their favorite movie stars ... It wasn't until I got back to*

*our New York office that I saw Mr. MacGregor again, and I forgot
to ask him how he ever got down.*

Benchley had an unhappy personal life, dying of alcoholism while
saying that his true ambition was to write a biography of Queen Anne.

Another top humorist of the time was S. J. Perelman, who also
wrote for the Marx Brothers. Perelman and Benchley were opposites
as stylists; where Benchley was the Hemingway of humorists—spare
and straightforward, the leanness of his prose setting off the improb-
abilities within—Perelman was florid, polysyllabic, and took delight
in literary acrobatics.

*"Have a bit of the wing, darling?" queried Diana solicitously, indi-
cating the roast Long Island airplane with applesauce . . . Soon we
were exchanging gay banter over the mellow Vouvray, laughing as
we dipped fastidious fingers into the Crisco parfait for which Diana
was famous.*

*Our meal finished, we sauntered into the play-room and Diana
turned on the radio. With a savage snarl the radio turned on her
and we slid over the waxed floor in the intricate maze of the jack-
daw strut.*

Rejected by McHale's Navy

As for long-form prose, there's really only one choice for greatest
comic novel of the last century: Joseph Heller's *Catch-22*. Heller was a
Mad Man, in the TV sense—he was working at an advertising agency
when he thought of a great first line for a novel. He wrote the last line
eight years later.

Catch-22 is many things—brutal, profane, amoral, kaleidoscopic,
hallucinogenic—but mostly hilarious, reveling in its clear-eyed cyni-
cism. It embraces the contradictions that make its hero, a bombardier
stationed off the Italian coast in the final months of World War II,

hate everything about his life yet want desperately to live. Which is difficult because he's in a situation where, as he points out, complete strangers are shooting at him.

I remember the first time I read the trial of Capt. Clevinger, featuring prosecutor Lieut. Scheisskopf (Yiddish for "shithead"). I was a teenager reading at a swimming pool, and everyone stared as I hooted · helplessly at the following:

> *"Just what the hell did you mean, you bastard, when you said we couldn't punish you?"* . . .
>
> *"I didn't say you couldn't punish me, sir."*
>
> *"When?" asked the Colonel.*
>
> *"I'm sorry, sir. I'm afraid I don't understand your question."*
>
> *"When didn't you say we couldn't punish you?"* . . .
>
> *"I never said you couldn't punish me."*
>
> *"Now you're telling us when you did say it. I'm asking you to tell us when you didn't say it."*
>
> *Clevinger took a deep breath. "I always didn't say you couldn't punish me, sir."*

After *Catch-22* was published, Heller tried to make some money in TV. He wrote two scripts for the sitcom *McHale's Navy*—like *Catch-22*, a World War II military comedy—of which one was produced and the other rejected.

Later in Heller's life someone said to him that he'd never written anything as good as *Catch-22*, to which he replied, "Who has?" He was right.

10

Invisible Rabbits and Fresh Fruit

HARVEY/A THOUSAND CLOWNS

Americans relish their free spirits, from corrupt cops to wisecracking wits to baleful bombardiers. So another American archetype is the Iconoclast—the nonconformist who stands up to authority. This ideal appeals to a broad political spectrum: conservatives love Ayn Rand's John Galt, liberals love John Steinbeck's Tom Joad. But in a way, these characters' beliefs are less important than their attitude: a jut-jawed refusal to be cowed, or be one of the crowd.

Two plays provide perfect examples of this: *Harvey* (1944) and *A Thousand Clowns* (1962). Both have nonconformist leads but they're very different, reflecting the differences in their times.

In Mary Chase's *Harvey*, Elwood P. Dowd's belief in a six-foot invisible rabbit is quiet and unaggressive. As America entered an era that would prize conformity, Dowd's strangeness is almost as invisible as his friend—other than his eccentric belief, he seems like anyone else.

But the play shows how Dowd's simple, unswerving faith in something no one else can see is acutely upsetting to the social order, to the point where he's committed to an asylum. He's saved by a psychiatrist—the ultimate rationalist of mid-twentieth-century America—who recognizes Dowd's belief as at worst harmless and at best transcendent.

Believer

In a time of surface normality that nonetheless contained the first stirrings of frightening societal threats like Communism and beatniks, *Harvey* said that nonconformists might see something other people don't, something not subversive but spiritual, something that can bring happiness if we only believe.

Almost twenty years later, *A Thousand Clowns* featured another iconoclast with a more explicitly political message. Murray Burns is a TV comedy writer who's skipped Timothy Leary's later admonition to tune in and turn on and gone straight to drop out; he's quit his job and decided to live life as a whim, which includes raising his twelve-year-old nephew Nick.

Fruit

Murray's decision to leave the rat race is presented as heroic, so bold as to be profoundly disturbing to the people around him, who all represent conventional society. The world can't function, they say, if people act like Murray, but the play seems to be on Murray's side, the side of a pre-hippie ethos of "If it feels good, do it."

Most modern reviews of *A Thousand Clowns* call it dated in venerating a man who really *is* irresponsible. But the playwright, Herb Gardner, inserted a key character who opposes Murray and isn't a fool.

Arnold Burns is a talent agent who visits his brother each day offering fresh fruit, which Murray takes, and job interviews, which Murray doesn't. Murray thinks Arnold's thrown his life away, giving up his freedom for money, and Arnold thinks Murray's throwing away not just his own life but Nick's. We know whose side the play is on; Murray's the romantic rebel, Arnold a conventional conformist. Most important, Murray's funny and charming, as in his description to social workers of the way Nick came into his life . . .

See link 14: Murray relates how his sister left her son with him while she went for a pack of cigarettes then returned six years later; how her philosophy of life "falls somewhere to the left of Whoopee!"; and that she now communicates "primarily by rumor."

But for all the ways in which Murray seems an enlightened free spirit, the play keeps showing how he falls short as a friend, a brother, a father, a human being. He's not really so different from his sister, living a carefree life oblivious to its effect on others. To illustrate the alternative, Gardner gives Murray's businessman brother a speech so unexpected and stirring that it won an Oscar for Martin Balsam in the movie version.

Fed up with being called a sellout, Arnold extols the nobility of "getting along":

> *I am not an exceptional man, so it is possible for me to stay with things the way they are . . . I have a talent for surrender. [But] you cannot convince me that I am one of the Bad Guys. I get up, I go, I lie a little, I peddle a little, I watch the rules, I talk the talk. We fellas have those offices high up there so we can catch the wind and go with it, however it blows. But, and I will not apologize for it, I take pride; I am the best possible Arnold Burns.*

If the criticism of *A Thousand Clowns* is that its hero represents simplistic, unrealistic rebellion, how do we explain that speech, which says that sometimes the bravest thing a person can do is conform—that is, be realistic, work within the system, and find happiness not in some romanticized escape from responsibility but in the modest graces of work, compromise, and fresh fruit.

11

More Even More History of Ha!

MUSIC HALLS TO VAUDEVILLE

When we left the history of comedy, it was killing Abraham Lincoln. But let's not judge too harshly—comedy has also given employment to pigs.

As elite theater in England became more rambunctious, public entertainment loosened up too; women were allowed to act, bringing in a wider range of audience. But class war is a revered British tradition, and by the nineteenth century there was a new form of entertainment for the lower classes—*music hall*, a kind of variety theater that in America became *vaudeville*.

While Lincoln was getting sockdogolized (sorry—too soon?), music halls in Europe and England (where Charlie Chaplin later learned his skills) showcased novelty acts that fascinated the masses and revolted the gentry.

Ricky Jay, the renowned magician and expert on cards and con games, is also a scholar of specialty acts—his book *Learned Pigs and Fireproof Women* is a fascinating survey of novelty performers of the last two hundred years, including:

☞ Harry Kahne, The Multiple Mental Marvel, who could write five different words simultaneously with pieces of chalk in each hand, each foot, and his mouth;

☞ Toby, The Amazing Pig of Knowledge, who could add numbers, guess cards, and wrote his autobiography;

☞ Arthur Lloyd, the Human Card Index, who could produce on demand virtually any printed item from his pockets;

☞ Matthew Buchinger, a magician, artist, and sharpshooter who played a half-dozen musical instruments, danced the hornpipe, and was twenty-nine inches high . . . with no feet, thighs or arms; and . . .

☞ Joseph Pujol, Le Petomane, whose musical odorless farts of popular melodies caused women to faint, although historians disagree about whether that was due to the beauty of his farting or the deadly combination of helpless laughter and tight corsets.

For the *lower* lower classes, music hall became *burlesque*. Originally a form of Greek farce in which women dressed like men to mock politicians and popular culture, burlesque used lots of theatrical traditions and styles, including music, dance, parody, social commentary, and of course, hot babes.

Beautiful

In England, burlesque was condemned by the elite for its sexuality and outspokenness and was hounded off the legitimate stage, relegated to saloons and barrooms, where it became mostly dirty jokes.

Damn Yankee

As these comic traditions hopped the pond, the US developed its first distinctly

American comic character: the Yankee, a gangly traveler who told tall tales, played practical jokes. was crafty, sly, often uneducated, but usually got the better of his betters . . . and then let them know it.

Yankee

Because the Yankee was the ultimate braggart, whether taming a blue ox or planting every apple tree in America, he never let you forget his prowess.

Echoes of the Yankee come through all American entertainment history, right up to rappers: the cocky, swaggering boaster who's got more money, women, cars, gold teeth, and floor space than you. Mark Twain paints a portrait of a Yankee braggart in a sketch from *Life on the Mississippi*, adapted by actor William Mooney . . .

See link 15: "Half-horse, half-alligator," where the braggart claims, "I take nineteen alligators and a bar'l of whiskey for breakfast when I'm in robust health, and a bushel of rattlesnakes and a dead body when I'm ailing. I been sharpening up my thumbnail and I'm gonna go home with somebody's eyeball in my pocket."

Americans have always loved bragging about themselves and trashing you. "Yankee Doodle" was a British ditty lampooning Americans, but after winning the battle of Bunker Hill we adopted it as a theme song and, in a kind of comedic judo, rewrote the lyrics to insult the English.

American slaves had their own form of braggadocio, which went by a few different names: toasting, signifying, "the dozens." A game of one-upsmanship using tall tales and insults, it was a forerunner of rap.

Another American comic archetype is the opposite of the brash Yankee: the Innocent—the rube who wins out because his comic Goodness protects him and foils foes. It's a beguiling persona but comedically challenging because it's inherently passive. In silent film, Harold Lloyd (p. 17) and Harry Langdon were effective Innocents, while Chaplin and Keaton combined Rube and Yankee; though basically innocent, they do whatever it takes to win the day (i.e., save the girl).

The Innocent is still with us today: Steve Martin in *The Jerk*, Will Ferrell in *Elf*, Ben Stiller in, well, a lot. Groucho played both Rube and Innocent, running a real estate scam in *Coconuts* yet bamboozled by Chico in *A Day at the Races*; to get the inside dope on a horse race, Groucho ends up buying a tip sheet, a code book and a "breeder's guide" in five volumes.

Comedy to Go

Whether Innocent or con man, Americans are rootless and restless, so we adapted traditions like British Music Hall and took it on the road.

By the nineteenth century, thousands of *minstrel* and *medicine shows* travelled America with programs of comedy, music, jugglers, and novelty acts, while selling "miracle elixirs" like Coca Cola, named for the ingredient it shared with other so-called patent medicines: cocaine.

In the 1900s there were *Chautauqua Assemblies*—travelling tent shows that began as adult-education lectures and added entertainment. Around the same time, American burlesque became a populist blend of satire, broad comedy, and dancing girls. It competed with vaudeville and lost, devolving into striptease until a morals crackdown in the '30s led to its death.

Vaudeville—the word comes from fifteenth-century France and means "satirical song"—featured singing and dancing (popular and

classical), animals, "monologists," and novelties. Comedy acts sometimes used the old slap stick, now a goat bladder stretched on a board.
American vaudeville became the training ground for generations
of comics, from Buster Keaton to the Marx Brothers to Bob Hope.

If you're willing to try vaudeville without the goat bladder, there
are a number of '30s and '40s movies that show its more glamorous
form, as embodied by the Ziegfeld Follies.

A lavish Times Square spectacle of song, comedy, and dancers
"glorifying the American Girl," the Follies produced dozens of stars,
including Fannie Brice, W.C. Fields (who started as a juggler), and
Will Rogers (rope tricks).

In the late '20s, vaudeville began incorporating film shorts, thus
shooting itself in the foot. As vaudeville got killed off by the movies,
some performers moved to Jewish resorts in New York's Catskill
Mountains, an area that catered to so many Eastern European im-
migrant families it became known as the Borscht Belt.*

Many vaudevillians became *tummlers*, essentially hotel jesters, and
ended up stars with world-famous names like Yakov Maza, Joseph
Levitch, Milton Berlinger, Isaac Caesar, Leonard Schneider, Allan Konigsberg, David Kaminsky, and Melvin Kaminsky; otherwise known
as Jackie Mason, Jerry Lewis, Milton Berle, Sid Caesar, Lenny Bruce,
Woody Allen, Danny Kaye, and Mel Brooks.

Vaudeville limped on till the late '40s, when a new piece of technology put the last nail in its coffin. As Bob Hope said (in a line written
by Larry Gelbart), "When vaudeville died, television was the box
they put it in."

Before its death, vaudeville produced the most famous comedy
routine in history: Abbott and Costello's "Who's on First." Abbott's
a baseball manager and tells Costello about his team . . .

---

* A joke originated there about a woman who complained about the hotel
food: "Terrible, and such small portions."

See link 16: Abbott's team's unusual names cause Costello some confusion.

Nomenclature

12

The Jewish Question

The Borscht Belt was hardly the only part of America that saw significant Jewish immigration; in the early '40s, the cream of European culture fled the Nazis and landed in Los Angeles, the new home of playwright Bertold Brecht, novelist Thomas Mann, director Max Reinhardt, and writer/director Billy Wilder.

The first wave of these West Coast émigrés was German, which led to some tension with later arrivals. One evening, a crowd of Hungarian refugees were chattering to each other at a Santa Monica party and director Otto Preminger had enough; he slammed down his fist and said, "We're in America, damn it—speak German!"

In comedy, the impact of this influx was stupendous; by the '70s, it was estimated that Jews made up about 3 percent of the US population ... and 80 percent of professional comedians.

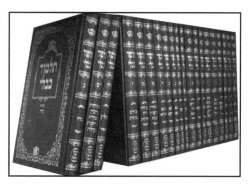

Funny: The Book: The Prequel

Their humor emerged from Jewish traditions. The Jewish holy book, the Talmud, uses intricate, elaborate arguments (parsing words—see *hermeneutics*, page 31) and absurd situations (think of the role of nonsense and whimsy in comedy) to tease out the meaning of religious dictates.

Jewish satire may have sprung from the egalitarian nature of Eastern European communities, where the powerful were mocked subtly rather than attacked overtly. There were even Jewish jesters: *badchonim* were hired for weddings to poke fun at prominent members of the community—they mocked rabbis, rulers, and rich people.

But the biggest influence on Jewish humor is Jewish history.

Oy

Irving Brecher, a comedy writer who did two Marx Brothers movies, said the only escape from persecution is laughter, to forget grief. Nobel Prize–winning novelist Saul Bellow said, "Oppressed people tend to be witty." Mel Brooks: "My comedy comes from the feeling that as a Jew, even though you're better and smarter, you'll never belong."

The often-tragic history of the Jewish people made them mordant, philosophical, ironic, introspective, sometimes bitter, but also playful, fanciful, and irreverent.

A man goes into a coffeehouse in Berlin in 1935 and sees a rabbi reading an anti-Semitic paper. He's horrified: "Why do you have that Nazi libel sheet? Are you some kind of masochist or a self-hating Jew?"

"Not at all. When I read the Jewish papers, I learn about pogroms, riots in Palestine, assimilation in America. But in this I see that Jews control the banks, dominate the arts, and are about to take over the world. It makes me feel better."

In a Russian shtetl, there was a rumor that a Christian girl had been murdered. Fearing a pogrom, everyone gathered at the synagogue.

Suddenly the rabbi rushed in yelling, "Wonderful news! The mur-
dered girl was Jewish!"

Bel Kaufman, the 101-year-old author of *Up the Down Staircase* and
granddaughter of famed Yiddish author Sholem Aleichem (his stories
about the milkman Tevye were the basis for *Fiddler on the Roof*), says
that because Jews have been objects of such hatred and scorn, their
humor is often a defense mechanism: "We'll talk about ourselves in
a more damaging way than you can."

Even Freud noted how Jews delight in mocking every aspect of
their own sensibility—their acute sense of suffering . . .

On her TV series, comic Sarah Silverman played a brainless, insen-
sitive version of herself who competes with her sister over who can
put on the best Holocaust memorial. "I'm gonna bury you," says
Sarah. "When this is over, you're gonna wish the Holocaust never
happened."

. . . the divisions within their religion . . .

An Orthodox, Conservative, and Reform rabbi debate whether one
should say a brokhe (blessing) over a lobster, shellfish being forbid-
den to observant Jews. The Conservative rabbi is baffled: "What
could you say?" The Orthodox rabbi asks, "What's a lobster?" The
Reform rabbi asks, "What's a brokhe?"

A shipwrecked Jew builds two temples on his tiny island. He's rescued
and asked, "Why do you have two temples?" He points and says,
"That one I don't go to."*

---

* In *Jewish Humor*, Joseph Telushkin claims he saw the same joke, considered
a classic of Jewish sensibility, in a book of *Welsh* jokes. The way I deal with this
revelation is to stick my fingers in my ears and go "la la la la la."

. . . even the world's stereotypes of them . . .

Question: What's a Jewish dilemma? Answer: Half-price pork.

Silverman referred to Chinese people as "Chinks" in a joke and there was an uproar:

They put my name in all the papers, calling me a racist. And it hurt, y'know? As a Jew, I'm really concerned that we're losing control of the media.

(She says, "I don't care if you think I'm racist—I just want you to think I'm thin.")

There's also the Zen-like . . .

Two Jewish ladies were sitting in a deli, minding their own business.

Slender Racist

That's the joke.

But while Jews' achievements have given them some degree of self-confidence, there's always Mel Brooks's sense of being an outsider, of not belonging; Groucho famously said, "I would never be a member of a club which would have me as a member." And as a corollary, Mort Sahl said, "If you can't join them, beat them."

Still, for all the importance of history and tradition, maybe humor's a genetic trait. In the '50s, Larry Gelbart was asked why so many comedy writers like him were young and Jewish and he answered, "Probably because our parents were old and Jewish."

The Immortal Allan Stewart Konigsberg

WOODY ALLEN

Not only is there no God, but try getting a plumber on weekends.
Some guy hit my fender and I told him, "Be fruitful and multiply."
But not in those words.
Women say I'm a great lover. That's 'cause I practice a lot when
I'm alone.

There's little doubt that when the history of American humor in the twentieth century is written, the preeminent Hebraic practitioner will be recognized as Allan Stewart Konigsberg, Woody Allen to you.

Allen's jokes are so recognizable that they seem to come with a copyright notice attached. Allen appeared in *The Front*, a 1976 movie about the McCarthy Era written by former blacklisted writer Walter Bernstein. When his character said, "In my family the only sin was to pay retail," everyone assumed was it Allen's line, even though Bernstein wrote it.

Allen's movies have received just a bit of critical attention, so

Immortal

let's concentrate on his other careers, as standup comic and prose writer.

He was born in New York City (who'da thunk, huh?) in 1935. As a teenager he wrote jokes for newspaper columnists and comics, but his big break was helping with shows at a socialist summer camp in the Borscht Belt, which led to his writing for Sid Caesar's TV show at the age of seventeen.

This was in the early '50s, when pop culture was redefining itself after the war, and Henny Youngman's "Take my wife, please" was being replaced by Nichols and May improvising a sketch about Albert Schweitzer to a Mozart piano concerto.

The new comics didn't just talk about themselves, home, and work; they tackled social issues, philosophy, psychoanalysis, and politics. It was the time of Lord Buckley, Lenny Bruce, and Mort Sahl (pp. 35–36), who inspired Allen to quit his job as a top TV writer and set out to become a standup. He was terrible—incredibly nervous, reading his material from pages clutched in his trembling hands while never looking at the audience.

Allen realized the key was finding a persona to put the jokes over and, more importantly, to write the jokes to. Like most comics, he chose to build on what was there, inventing a false autobiography from visible characteristics.

He used his shortness and glasses to create a variant of the classic Jewish *schlemiel*, or *schnook*: hapless, neurotic, a loser in life and love. (In fact, Allen was an athlete in school and, with his wit and intellect, never lacked for women.)

He began talking to the college kids that made up a large part of his audience in Greenwich Village almost like a teacher lecturing on the topic of what he'd been doing recently. Unlike Sahl and Bruce, his act was less about his view of the times than about how the times affected him.

He took Sahl's intelligence and refusal to pander, combined it with the early Bob Hope's jaunty cockiness, then added Jules Feiffer's psychological deconstruction of hipster personal relationships. He was aided in this by Freudian analysis, which he began in 1959 and continued for thirty years. One observer said his show sometimes "seemed less like a public performance than a private confession." But it was all, literally and figuratively, an act.

Allen disguised the intrinsic traditionalism of his standup—he almost never talked politics,* he made jokes about his personal life—with a conscious overlay of intellectualism and literary allusions that he admitted were essentially faked; though obviously bright, he failed in pretty much every educational environment he'd ever been in, including getting kicked out of two colleges after flunking Motion Picture Production.

As Allen became more confident, his persona did too, evolving from intellectual neohipster to swinger—or, as he would say it, "swin-**ger**," as his idiosyncratic overemphasis of consonants became a trademark.

In an early appearance with Johnny Carson, he told one of his great jokes: "Y'see this watch I'm wearing? I'm very proud of it. A gorgeous antique pocket watch and it means a lot to me. My grandfather, on his deathbed, sold me this watch." Carson practically fell off his chair, which in those days meant your ascension into Comedy Olympus.

Allen also spoke about a traumatic incident from his youth . . .

See link 17: Allen tells how he was kidnapped, whereupon his parents "snapped into action" by renting his room.

"I'll Put Mr. Allen On"

With his success in movies Allen quit standup, though for a long time, lines in his films could easily have come from his act. But his

---

* Allen delved into politics once, in a mock documentary about a mock Henry Kissinger character, made for PBS in 1972 but never shown. Talking about Nixon's Attorney General, the narrator says John Mitchell "has many ideas for strengthening the country's law enforcement methods and is hampered only by lack of funds and the Constitution."

cultural standing seemed to diminish after the 1992 Soon-Yi/Mia Farrow scandal.

In the previous decade Allen had moved from being a clever quipster to a probing ethical analyst. Though never explicitly moralistic he wrestled with the big questions of life, superficially in his standup, then earnestly in movies like *Crimes and Misdemeanors*. Allen never preached, but he made it clear that he took right and wrong very seriously.

When he had an affair with his girlfriend's daughter, it was as though he betrayed us (or at least, himself). The man who'd faced God and death with quips showing his fear that one didn't exist and the other did was suddenly like everyone else, hiding behind dubious actions with airy self-centeredness. "The heart wants what it wants," he said by way of explanation, but some people questioned if he was referencing the actual organ involved.

Still, outrage at learning that Woody Allen was human, fallible, and susceptible to temptation said more about us than him. One way to have known that would be to listen to his standup act. Here's Allen in 1966 on the subject of ethics; he gets a call from a guy who asks if he'll do a vodka ad . . .

> I said, "No. I'm an artist, I do not do commercials. I don't pander. I don't drink vodka, and if I did I wouldn't drink your product." And the guy says, "Too bad—it pays $50,000." And I said, "Hold on. I'll put Mr. Allen on the phone."

Pursued by a Verb

It's a simplification with some truth in it to say that Allen's comic work consists of one overriding joke, the contrast between the cosmic and the mundane: "I don't believe in an afterlife, although I am bringing a change of underwear."

But Allen's range is revealed in his dazzling, breathtakingly inventive, and linguistically precise prose pieces. He assumes an audience as literate and neurotic as he is, and his topics range across terrain similar to his early movies—politics, culture, history, cosmology, sex, and death.

Allen, who once said, "My one regret in life is that I'm not someone else," melds the confidence and fluidity of S. J. Perelman and the whimsy of Robert Benchley into a unique and distinctive style.

In "The Whore of Mensa," we meet a genius-IQ call girl who'll discuss Melville for money, either *Moby Dick* or the shorter novels, "symbolism's extra," and responds to your insights by moaning "Oh yes, baby, that's deep." She also sells emotional experiences—for a hundred she'll lend you her Bartok records and let you watch while she has an anxiety attack.

In "My Speech to the Graduates," Allen intones that "More than any other time in history, humanity is at a crossroads: one path leads to despair and utter hopelessness; the other, to total extinction. Let us pray we have the wisdom to choose correctly."

Allen's story "Mr. Big" has a Barnard sophomore hiring a private dick to find God so she can ace her Philosophy final . . .

See link 18: The girl, pseudonymously "Heather Buttkiss," is said to have a figure "which described a set of parabolas that could cause cardiac arrest in a yak."

Allen's most famous piece, "The Kugelmass Episode," has a married man confessing his temptation to cheat to his therapist, who warns there's no instant cure for that compulsion: "I'm an analyst," he says, "not a magician." So Kugelmass quits therapy and hires a magician, who projects him into the novel *Madame Bovary*, where he and Emma have a torrid affair. "My God, I'm doing it with Madame Bovary," he says in amazement. "Me, who failed freshman English."

Emma wants to see Manhattan so Kugelmass takes her out of the book, which is noticed by a Stanford literature professor who nonetheless accepts the appearance of a twentieth-century Jewish New

Yorker in *Madame Bovary*, not to mention the disappearance of the title character, by noting that "the mark of a classic is that you can read it a thousand times and always find something new."

Not surprisingly, complications ensue and the hero ends up projected into a Spanish textbook "running for his life over barren, rocky terrain as the word *tener* ('to have')—a long and hairy irregular verb—raced after him on its spindly legs."

Woody Allen will always be remembered, no doubt a source of intense frustration to the man who once said, "I don't want to achieve immortality through my work—I want to achieve it through not dying."

14

There Is No Chapter 14

Really. There just isn't.

And it's too late to get a refund.

15

Why We Laugh . . .
Or Do We?*

THE EVOLUTION OF HA!

We've all faced that awkward question from a child: "Mommy, Daddy—where does comedy come from?" It's not as difficult to explain as babies, but ironically, the answer's the same: when a man and a woman love each other very much, they get drunk, screw, and pass out. The result is either a baby or a funny story.

Let's look for the origins of funny, after first agreeing to separate the biological phenomenon of laughter from the psychology of humor. Do you agree? If so, send a self-addressed, stamped envelope to "Mischy" c/o this publisher.

You better agree, because laughter and humor do just fine without each other. Our yucks are so unpredictable and illogical that they can be a response to things that are exact opposites . . .

We laugh because something's familiar and at things we've never seen; when others laugh and when others don't;** at something funny and at something sad.*** We're a species that finds amusement in

---

* Title courtesy of Robert Benchley.
** The musical number "Springtime for Hitler" in Mel Brooks's *The Producers* leaves its Broadway audience aghast, while we howl.
*** In the sitcom episode generally considered TV's greatest, "Chuckles Bites The Dust" from *The Mary Tyler Moore Show*, Mary's unable to stop laughing during a funeral until the priest says the deceased—a clown—would have welcomed her merriment, causing Mary to sob miserably.

children playing and not long ago (humorist Stephen Potter points out), in "a lunatic on the end of a chain or a bear tied to a post and bitten to death by dogs." (Guess you had to be there.) We laugh from sheer joy and we laugh in sheer despair.

Monkey Urine: The Foundation of Comedy

Laughter not only doesn't need humor, it doesn't need humans.

Dian Fossey and Jane Goodall tickled gorillas. That's not actually relevant to this discussion, it's graffiti I saw in a bathroom.

No, it's true. The anthropologists then observed "repetitive vocalizations in response to pleasure stimuli"—i.e., monkey yucks.

Primate amusement is well documented. Baby chimps react to human tickling with a "play face"—mouth open, upper teeth covered, lower teeth bared, panting sound on inward and outward breaths (all of which I do when I see a plasma TV under $300).

And it's not just chimps yucking it up—rats make an ultrasonic chirp when tickled and like it so much they come back for more. So

Rib-tickler

that's another way this book is invaluable in today's difficult economy: where else would you hear that jobs are available in the rat-tickling industry?

One theory of laughter is that ha-ha evolved from pant-pant. Because primates love pleasure-center brain stimulation, scientists speculate that the first action to produce laughter was the fake tickle.

But since laughter and humor don't always go together, is there evidence that monkeys actually have a sense of humor, preferably evidence in the form of body waste?

Funny you should ask. A researcher put the famous sign-language chimp Washoe on his shoulders, whereupon Washoe urinated down his back while making the sign for "funny." After which the researcher made the sign for "Good luck living till lunch when I throw you back in the jungle."

Terror: The Foundation of Comedy

If monkeys smile and laugh, we can assume Early Man did too; discounting the likelihood of paleolithic Back-Pee Festivals, the question is why.

Some scientists believe human smiling began as a failed scary-face. Let's say you're a Neanderthal—and I mean that in the best possible way—strolling by the local primordial swamp. Suddenly you see a Hominid, which is really weird 'cause didn't they die out like a million years ago? You bare your teeth but just as you're about to attack, run away, or soil yourself (I traditionally choose the third option), you see it's your brother-in-law. Your terrifying scowl stops halfway: "Bernie!" you yell happily, "I've invented smiling!" (Though being a Neanderthal, it comes out "Grghwrl! Shnsh bwng mlgzhr!")

Human laughter's origins may be in the threat-response instinct. Early Man sees a woolly mammoth charging and prepares to scream the alarm to his tribe. Then the mammoth slips and falls (not uncommon during the Ice Age), causing E. M.'s grimace of fear to become a wide smile and his scream of alarm to become a guffaw. Laughter, then, represents the release of tension when a perceived threat suddenly disappears.

With our increasingly sophisticated brains and decreasing exposure to mammoths, the concept of "threat" changes; now, a story that seems pointless but resolves in a surprising twist can be perceived as a "threat"—to order, logic, reason—that unexpectedly turns benign. Our more advanced brains see "danger" as incongruity and mystery; laughter represents our happy surprise when the danger passes, when the mystery resolves.

There may be biological evidence for a symbiotic relationship between danger and laughter; neurological experiments indicate that the circuitry that handles laughter in the human brain developed alongside the pathways for fear, and fear's cause: pain. When brain-damaged patients with a particular type of insular cortex injury are jabbed in the finger with a needle, they find it not painful but comical.

Of course, it all depends how you jab. Some people just jab funny.

Make Yucks Not War

As human societies developed, threats to survival came more from conflict than from predators or starvation. One theory says laughter developed from "the roar of triumph in a jungle duel"; the winner's family and buddies joined in and laughing became the signal that it was okay to relax. And as people snickered at the loser's black eye and broken arm, injury or deformity came to suggest that someone had been or could be defeated in battle. (This is a version of page 133's "Superiority Theory of Laughter," which sounds better than the "Nyah Nyah Nyah Theory of Obnoxious Jeering.")

At some point, laughter evolved from response to strategy. Jane Goodall observed a beta male challenge a pack's alpha male for an ovulating female. (Mmmm—ovulating female gorilla . . .) Presumably realizing he'd made a possibly fatal mistake, beta male thought of a way out; he laughed ("Kidding, just kidding—I don't even *like* ovulating females").

Then came the important part. Recognizing that the loss of the beta would deprive the tribe of a valuable adult male, the other chimps laughed too, defusing the crisis without violence. Chimp families that employed stratagems like group glee to avoid destructive in-fighting presumably outlasted ones that didn't.

Another theory says that laughter is a favored evolutionary trait because it indicates cognitive prowess (playwright Tom Stoppard calls it "the sound of comprehension"); in other words, people with good senses of humor are more sexually attractive. And I'd appreciate it if someone would go back to 1972 and tell that to Dawn Holloway.

16

That Wacky Existentialism

STEVE MARTIN

Even for the tiny minority of standups who become famous, life as a comic means years and years of grueling work, although at least the pay is bad. So why do they do it? Jerry Seinfeld tells a story which goes something like this:

> In the 1950s, Glenn Miller's band was touring when their small plane got engine trouble and had to land a few miles from their gig. Everyone grabbed their instruments and started to walk.
>
> It had been raining and as they crossed a muddy field, they saw a little house, and they stopped to look in the window.
>
> A family was inside, sitting at a table, fire blazing. Two kids, two loving parents, big meal . . . a perfect Norman Rockwell scene.
>
> The musicians are outside, soaking wet, exhausted. One of them looks in, shakes his head and says, "How can people live like that?"

In other words, you do it 'cause you love it.

Reading the Phone Book

When Woody Allen moved into movies, he left behind a standup scene with an identity crisis. For younger comics, there was no going back to the world of Vegas-style comedy. While Carlin and Pryor followed in Lenny Bruce's footsteps, a new generation of performers like Robert Klein and Albert Brooks found their audiences in unconventional venues like rock concerts and folk coffeehouses.

The comedy world was so dead that in 1976, a magazine named me Best Comedian in Boston. It takes away from this glorious honor only a little that at the time I was the *only* comedian in Boston. (Soon there was another, a kid named Jay Leno. I became #2.)

By the early '80s, the '60s Generation decided it was ready for a laugh and standup boomed, aided by clubs like LA's aptly named Comedy Store, which made showcasing comics—one after another all night long—a retail business.

There were stoner acts like Cheech and Chong, idiosyncratic talents like the professionally furious Sam Kinison (a less political version of today's Lewis Black), and Steven Wright with his cerebral one-liners: "You can't have everything. Where would you put it?"

There were conceptual performers like Brooks, who tested the saying that a great comic could get laughs reading the phone book by going on *The Tonight Show* and reading the phone book . . . while dropping his pants to reveal flowered boxer shorts. (Johnny Carson was not amused.)

Andy Kaufman often took it as a point of pride to *not* get laughs, reading from *The Great Gatsby* or watching his laundry spin in a portable dryer till the audience yelled him off the stage.

Postmodern metacomedy was intellectually stimulating but not very commercial. For that, some Boomer needed to blend conceptual humor with a persona and attitude that encompassed the post-Vietnam desire to escape politics and embrace, well, ourselves.

The Hilarity of Pointlessness

If you had to pick one world belief system as a comic sensibility, what would it be?

Try religion: Buddhism's got a fat guy—fat guys are funny. Catholicism, the men in charge wear dresses—drag always works. Philosophy—Utilitarianism, whatever's funniest to the most people. Logical Positivism . . . I won't even attempt a joke.

Hey, how about Existentialism? Meaninglessness, nothingness, pointlessness—that's gotta be funny, right?

Of course not. And yet in the late '60s, a young guy in Southern California took a psychology class at Cal State Long Beach and decided Existentialism was comedy gold.

Steve Martin's parents loved comedy, and as a kid he took in Laurel and Hardy, Amos 'n' Andy, Abbott and Costello, Bob Hope, Steve Allen, Jerry Lewis, and satirical songwriter Tom Lehrer.

He got a summer job selling guides at Disneyland, then worked in the park magic shop, learning card tricks, rope tricks, juggling, and how to make balloon animals and play the banjo.

Existential

But what really changed his life was that college class . . .

I read a treatise on comedy explaining that a laugh was formed when the storyteller created tension, then, with the punch line, released it . . . What if I created tension and never released it? What if I headed for a climax, but all I delivered was an anticlimax? What would the audience do with all that tension? . . . If I [denied] them the formality of a punch line, the audience would eventually pick their own place to laugh, essentially out of desperation.

Martin dropped out of school and wrote for the Smothers Brothers among others, then, like Woody Allen, decided to do or die as a standup. Initially his act was conventional, but he began thinking about the tyranny of punchlines; how their rhythm—setup/punchline, setup/punchline—almost forces the audience to laugh . . . which is, of course, the point of the rhythm.

And that's what gave Martin his breakthrough: don't tell the audience what's funny, let them find it on their own.

He decided to put together an act without jokes, and if it turned out to be an act without laughs, he'd never let the audience think he was failing but rather that something funny had happened that they hadn't figured out yet.

> *I would do my act without pausing for laughs; everything would either be delivered in passing, or the opposite—an elaborate presentation that climaxed in pointlessness.*

An elaborate presentation that climaxes in pointlessness; I'd like to have been there when he pitched that to his agent. Given that Martin was broke and going nowhere, it was pretty gutsy to think that an act different from anything anyone had ever done could be commercial. When he first tried it and audiences didn't laugh, Martin says he wanted to yell, "Wait, let me explain my theory!"

But he wasn't there yet. Like Allen, he knew he couldn't succeed without a clear and compelling persona, which he put together from pieces of his life: the Disneyland magic shop sold arrow-through-the-head novelty gags; a friend brought in a postcard showing the bottom of the legs of a couple having sex, labeled "Happy Feet"; the manager of a shop in Adventureland had a favorite saying—"Well excuse me for livin'!" And through it all ran Martin's observations of the fatuously self-involved Me Generation.

What's unique about Martin is that while comics like Benny, Hope, and Berle would invent quirks (cheapness, cowardice, lechery), their actual personalities weren't so different from their personas: Benny was low-key, Hope a wise-ass, Berle brash and loud. A perfect example is Groucho: the walk is fake, the moustache is fake, the personality pretty much the same.

Martin's unusual in having a persona radically different from his actual temperament. While we can assume Mr. Martin has his antic moments, by all accounts he's calm and serious, though witty, in private life. But onstage, Martin became the Wild and Crazy Guy and that helped his act be, at least superficially, just as wild and crazy.

Most comics try to give the impression they're flowing, albeit loosely, from topic to topic, using their stage personas to shape what are actually unconnected, self-contained bits. Martin didn't try to tie anything together, becoming instead something like the ringmaster for a collection of different acts: banjo player, juggler, clown, poet. And there's some *tummler* in there—the guy at the Catskills hotel determined to get everyone in the act.

The Greatest Performance

Like Robin Williams, Martin used planned spontaneity. Robin's head is full of bits, lines, and reactions that he takes out in different orders for different shows. But while he has a deep well of material that can fit any situation, Robin's not only willing but anxious to free-associate (though he'll pull out one of the old faces, voices, or bits if he gets in trouble—he even had a routine about not getting laughs for when he didn't get laughs).

While Martin seldom improvised, he shared Robin's comedy God: the unexpected. Although all humor is based on surprise, what's a working condition for most standups was sacrament to Martin. Using as few jokes or punchlines as any comic ever, nothing could be predictable—even if you'd seen him before, there was no way to know what he'd do next. And taking a page from the Pythons, he made his act simultaneously smart and stupid.

Sometimes he'd open by saying, "I have decided to make this the greatest performance of my life. Oh, wait, that's tomorrow night." He'd say, "I have a weird sexual fetish—I like wearing men's underwear." He'd ask, "How many people here tonight have never raised their hands before . . ."

One night he had a college audience leave the theater, go to an empty pool, and "swim" him over their heads. Another time he brought the audience to McDonald's, ordered three hundred hamburgers, then changed it to one order of fries.

Some of his greatest moments were on *Saturday Night Live* in the '70s . . .

See link 19: *Martin does a routine which includes his attempt to inhale a stool through a straw. (Upon failing, he says "Oh darn.")*

While most American comics—indeed, most American entertainers—are variants of the Yankee or Innocent archetypes, people like Martin and Williams are more elemental, going back to Trickster, the unpredictable upender of social convention and linear expectations.

The pleasure that archetype brings is singularly different than what we get from standard entertainment—with a Trickster onstage, being an audience is almost physical exertion, a session of endorphin-infused cranial aerobics as the brain tries to keep up, fabricating paths and bridges between the fireworks.

Like Martin theorized, material that isn't a joke in the conventional sense has to be shaped into humor inside our brains. The laugh comes not because there's a setup and punchline but because what we've heard is so clearly *not* a standard joke that it's up to us to find what to laugh at, when, and even why.

That's why Martin's act was postmodern. He constructed the humor, but the audience was responsible for "realizing" it, in both senses of the word—by understanding it, we make it real. Martin changed the contract of audience and comic, making the funny dependent on a charged symbiosis between them.

In a way Martin was the standup equivalent of Andy Warhol, who said, "I'm an artist, I did it, now it's your job to figure out why it's art." By never allowing our assumptions to be comfortably fulfilled, Martin got us to collaborate in creating our own laughter. (Author Arthur Koestler: "The artist rules his subjects by turning them into accomplices.")

Martin would take balloons, feverishly twist them together, then hold up the incoherent result and cry exultantly, "A dog!" Now making incomprehensible balloon animals is not intrinsically funny; if you see it at a street fair, it's just sad. Only by the audience bringing a wealth of associations to that moment—bad clowns, Martin's persona's blithely stupid confidence, our own subconscious but strangely compelling desire for the mish-mash of balloons to contain a recognizable shape—only then can a meaning emerge; the meaning being an exaltation of meaninglessness, an elaborate presentation that climaxes in pointlessness and, magically, makes comedy.

17

Me and My Dopamine

THE SCIENCE OF HA!

Everyone who's ever laughed at Steve Martin has the same question: is there any scientific basis behind it?

The answer is simple. Unfortunately, no one knows what it is.

We *do* know that despite the evidence from Ms. Goodall's giggling gorillas (p. 86), laughter doesn't come only from monkey-skin-saving desperation. It also depends on something the human brain's really good at: pattern recognition. Only by recognizing the underlying shape or rhythm of a joke or funny story can we be taken by surprise when the rhythm's interrupted or the pattern altered.

Evolutionary theorist Alastair Clarke:

An ability to recognize patterns instantly and unconsciously has proved a fundamental weapon in the cognitive arsenal of humans. The humorous reward has encouraged the development of such faculties, leading to the unique perceptual and intellectual abilities of our species.

Meaning that at a certain level, finding things funny requires brains. (This does not apply to body-switch movies.)

The method by which this mental facility can summon forth comedy is the subject of scientific disquisition by Monty Python entitled "Ribaldry: The Dispatch of an Edible Missile" . . .

See link 20: *The Pythons artfully throw pies.*

The whole point of that sketch—the whole point of comedy—is to play with our recognition of and desire for patterns. While watching Pythons with pies, we use our pattern-recognition skills to guess what they'll do next, even as we suspect it won't be what we expect.

The weird thing is that the state of knowing we don't know how the pattern will be altered isn't frustrating or irritating but pleasurable—as we try to figure out what'll happen, suspecting our guess will be wrong, our *confusion itself* feels good.

The reason for that is *dopamine*, a chemical called a "neurotransmitter", which helps the brain control emotions; when we feel happy, we get a shot of it right in the ol' nucleus accumbens. (My patent for dopamine-flavored Brussels sprouts is pending.)

Dopamine is critical to pattern recognition because after a pattern is established (a rat gets a cracker when a bell rings, a series of monocled

plutocrats slip on banana peels), the brain reacts at the trigger (appearance of cracker, dropping of peel), giving us a dose of sweet, sweet dopamine in anticipation of the pleasure to come. If the pattern changes, the brain sends out an adrenaline-drenched electrical signal ("error-related negativity") warning us that because something unexpected happened, we need to pay attention:

Just add adrenaline

"React, dammit!" And we do, with excitement, fear . . . or laughter.

Comedy is about generating that signal, getting the audience drunk (or in nightclubs, drunker) on a delicious dopamine/adrenaline cocktail. And the key to doing that is deception.

Scientists in Artificial Intelligence teach computers to understand jokes with a principle called "Violated Expectations" (a concept that goes back to Hobbes, Kant, Pascal, and even Cicero). That's because comedy works like a con game—get 'em to think you'll do/say one thing, then do something else. And that something else is by definition a form of nonsense in that it violates expectations, "doesn't make sense."

But comedy only happens when the brain recognizes it's been fooled. So why does humor even exist? If that knock-knock joke tricked you, shouldn't you be angry? ("'Orange you glad I didn't say banana?' How dare you, sir!")

A theory out of Tufts University says the brain uses humor as a bribe to keep us monitoring our information intake: I hear a joke; figure out the mistaken assumption that fooled me; feel depressed at my stupidity for a nanosecond; then get a delightful reward of laughter that encourages me to keep examining my assumptions.

Giving your nucleus accumbens a workout doesn't just feel good, it may make you smarter; research indicates we learn better after being exposed to humor,* or even just nonsense. Searching for patterns is like calisthenics for the brain. So that Python clip just got you four IQ points—you're welcome.

When you combine pattern recognition with a trusted source, you can get an illogical response. Milton Berle inserted meaningless phrases into jokes and discovered that the audience laughed anyway. When Bob Hope toured England, Larry Gelbart wrote him a joke about a motel. It got a roar but Gelbart remembered something; he asked his British date, "Do you know what a motel is?" "No." "Then why did you laugh?" "I don't know. Bob Hope is funny."

Laughter: The Best/Worst Medicine

Laughing at nothing isn't always due to pattern recognition or great comics. In Tanganyika in 1962, a schoolgirl told a joke to a friend, they

---

* Jews (naturally) have always known this—the Talmud says that the third-century sage Rabbah opened all his lessons with a joke.

started giggling uncontrollably, laughter spread to the other kids, then the teachers, and the school had to close. Laughter then went through the entire village to the neighboring towns, becoming so severe that fourteen schools closed, a thousand people were affected, and the laughter plague lasted for two-and-a-half years.

And then there are the people who die laughing. Really: writer Thomas Urquhart in 1660, after hearing Charles II had become King of England; a man seeing Neil Simon's first play; a fifty-year-old bricklayer who, while watching a British TV show, laughed for twenty-five continuous minutes then expired—his widow sent a letter to the show with thanks for making his final moments so happy.

Laughter can be deadly, but *not* laughing can be torture—literally. Author Lawrence Weschler says that in the '80s, Uruguayan political prisoners would be forced to watch a comedy film knowing they'd be tortured if they laughed. (The human need to laugh supports Freud's "Relief" theory, page 137.)

The Pythons also provide an example of this; in *Life of Brian*, Pontius Pilate—afflicted with a speech impediment—is surprised to hear the name of one of his best friends become a source of amusement to his impertinent guards . . .

See link 21: Pilate forbids his guards to laugh at the name of his friend Biggus Dickus.

But generally, laughing's good for you—emotionally, intellectually, even physically. It is, after all, a form of exercise, working fifteen separate facial muscles and everything from the vocal cords to the heart to the abdominals (with luck, stopping before the sphincter). It's estimated that a hearty laugh is equivalent to ten minutes of aerobics, meaning the expression "a hearty laugh" should be taken literally.

A sixteenth-century educator wrote that laughter cured colds, headaches, and melancholy, suggesting that "Parties which desire it can suffer themselves to be tickled under the armpittes," a practice that now costs $200 in the East Village. (I priced it, I never paid.)

Laugh!

"A merry heart doeth good like a medicine," says no less an authority than God (Proverbs 17:22). The University of Haifa offers a degree in Medical Clowning, and studies show that women who see clowns on the day they receive in vitro fertilization are more likely to become pregnant, presumably because laughter lessens the stress of the procedure. (Leaving the question of incredibly virile clowns unexplored.)

When author Norman Cousins was diagnosed with a rare connective tissue disease and given months to live, he developed a recovery program that consisted of massive doses of Vitamin C and the Marx Brothers:

> *I made the joyous discovery that ten minutes of belly laughter had an anesthetic effect and would give me at least two hours of pain-free sleep. When the pain-killing effect of the laughter wore off, we would switch on the motion picture projector [and] it would lead to another pain-free interval.*

So laughter doesn't just make you smarter—it cures all diseases.

Well maybe not all, but it's been shown to increase endorphins, pain tolerance, production of T-cells and oxygen levels in the brain, and to lower blood sugar, alleviate stress, and provide critical employment opportunities for kids who spent high school getting beaten up and never having sex.

I am *not* talking about myself.

Okay, I am.

Laughter's health benefits were clearly established by a 1992 study showing that children laugh up to three hundred times a day, adults less than twenty. This explains why young people live so much longer than old people.

Most of those twenty adult chortles aren't from anything funny: 80 to 90 percent of our everyday laughter is from people saying things like "I know" or "See ya later."*

Believing the body can't distinguish between real and fake merriment, a doctor in India started a "Laughter Club" in 1995; they're now in sixty-six countries, including six thousand in India—in Iran, the Tehran City Council's club has twenty thousand members. The Japanese spend billions of yen a year on "smiling schools"—better health through grinning—which means the people who run these clubs and schools are banking all the way to the laughs.

But for planned laughing to work, you gotta fake it for real. Scientists draw a distinction between "surface acting"—the forced smile of a date when you reveal you're on Charlie Sheen's Twitter feed—and "deep acting," where you make yourself happy through jolly thoughts; a study showed that fake smiling actually makes you feel worse. Still, genuine funny producing genuine laughs results in genuine health, meaning that comedy makes you brilliant, rich, and immortal.

---

* A man in a Monty Python sketch finds that whatever he says makes people laugh uncontrollably—"Good morning," "Not so warm today," everything. He tells a friend that his life is unbearable and he's going to commit suicide; his friend laughs uncontrollably.

18

Betty Lou Zombax

MORK AND MINDY

And yet after almost forty years in comedy, I'm maybe only two of those things. Wait, not two . . . what's the number I'm thinking of? Oh, that's right—none.

But I'm certainly older than I was, and those years of ~~wisdom~~ ~~experience~~ stuff give me some ~~fascinating insight~~ not-totally-lame stories about finding the funny.

My first job in TV was on *Mork and Mindy*, a spinoff from an episode of *Happy Days* about an alien living on earth. The guy originally cast was a Vegas comic named John Byner; on the third day of rehearsal, he quit, saying it was the stupidest role he'd ever had. Robin Williams was hired the next day and if you ever catch that episode of *Happy Days*, you'll see that his costume doesn't fit—he's wearing Byner's.

I got hired on the strength of a seven-page sketch (those were the days) and even though I'd been a standup, my act was mostly conceptual; I'd never really written a joke. Well, one: "I broke up with my girlfriend awhile ago. We had different religious beliefs; she was an atheist, and at the time, I thought I was God." Amusing perhaps, but not exactly sitcom material.

It turned out I had some facility for jokes, but getting my first episode on the air was torment. I struggled for days, weeks, trying to

Robin Williams and Pam Dawber

think of a story that wasn't too weird or too familiar.

Finally I got one. I pitched it to the producers and writing staff . . . and they liked it! I couldn't believe it. As I left the room, I turned to another writer, an older man (meaning fifteen years younger than I am now) who'd written for *All in the Family* and many other series.

"I'm so relieved," I said. "I was afraid you guys thought my story wouldn't work." "Oh we know it'll work," he said. "It worked on *Newhart*, it worked on *Taxi*, it worked on *Cheers* . . ."

That same writer had a telling anecdote. One season he wrote the Christmas episode of *All in the Family*, a prestigious gig, since holiday shows are the most-watched episodes of the year. He was visiting home when it aired and saw it with his parents. When it ended, his father turned to him and said, "Wonderful! But tell me, how does Carroll O'Connor think of all those funny things to say each week?"

Nowadays most people know the role screenwriters play. One of my happiest moments as a novice writer came in an episode where Mork goes to the post office thinking he has to register as an alien . . .

See link 22: Mork fills out a form: "Name—Mork. Education—P.S. One Million Six. Graduation date—Betty Lou Zombax."

That long, rolling laugh from the studio audience was a huge thrill for me, knowing that America was being entertained by a joke I'd made up in seventh grade.

Becoming One-Dimensional

Mork was one of the Garry Marshall armada of shows; in 1978, he created four of the top five series on TV. Garry wasn't entirely pleased with me at first. He called me into his office: "Misch, I read your script. It's witty."

"Uh, thanks?"

"No. We don't do witty. We do funny." Garry didn't want people chuckling with appreciation at the writer's cleverness—he wanted them to make the loud barking sound that resulted in his buying another house.

Once Robin got stuck with a bad line at the end of a scene and Garry decreed that from then on, every scene had to end with a door closing. What he meant was that the punctuation of a door slam would help the audience reaction, and if not, at least the actor wouldn't be left standing in the middle of the stage.

The problem was, the producers took what Garry said not metaphorically ("Come up with a better last line or have someone exit") but literally, and every scene for the next five shows—that's about thirty scenes—ended with someone leaving a room.

The legend of *Mork and Mindy* is that Robin ad-libbed everything. Well, there were ten people working till four in the morning writing those ad-libs.

The truth is, Robin was hilarious and a brilliant improviser, but a lot of his ad-libs consisted of grabbing his crotch and swearing, which couldn't get on TV. Most of what was aired was written, but Robin deserves the credit because the show wouldn't have been a hit with John Byner—Robin's faces, voices and physical comedy were what made him, and us, an overnight sensation.

He helped in less expected ways too. When one of our scripts had a minor character die of a heart attack, the network was horrified; way too dark for a sitcom, they said—couldn't the guy just faint or something? Robin saved us, refusing to let it be watered down: "There's no such thing," he said, "as gray comedy."

My biggest ally on the show was the only other writer under thirty, April Kelly, who shared my concern that every character other than Mork was a cliché. Mindy was supposed to be a typical American

The Author/The 70's

girl, but given that she had no friends, goals, neuroses, or income, she seemed to us more alien than Mork. We joked that she'd have to grow considerably in order to become one-dimensional.

The actress who played her, Pam Dawber, was a sweet person in a tough spot. She loved Robin and America loved her, but she knew, as *TV Guide* said, that there would be a considerable audience for a show called *Mork and Furniture*.

JLS

Once April and I were on deadline and couldn't find a joke, so we invented something that we later learned has been invented by pretty much every comedy writer who ever lived. We called ours "JLS": Joke-Like Substance. It's a line that looks like a joke, sounds like a joke, and acts like a joke—it gets a laugh—but isn't actually funny. Pattern recognition.

I think our first JLS had Mork saying, "It's like there's a panther in my pajamas." It fits the comedy benchmarks: it's got alliteration with hard consonants (p. 112), a vaguely dirty mental image (wild animal near someone's genitals), and it allows the star to do something funny physically. But it comes less from the feelings of a character than the needs (More Jokes!) of a writer.

Still, no matter how cynically a line was written, the combination of joke pattern and Robin Williams almost always got us laughs. Which was kind of discouraging and, ultimately, creatively corrupting.

I definitely lost my illusions on that show. Once, when we were hard up for a scene, we had Mindy talk about her dead mother. It was a real tearjerker, but April and I were unmoved; were we the only people in America who remembered there had never been a reference to Mindy's mother before that moment? I was standing near the audience as we filmed and heard someone say, "Whoa . . . They can do drama too."

Probably my favorite *Mork* moment happened in the writers' room. Years ago, that section of Paramount Studios had been RKO Studios; the *Mork* stage was used for *King Kong*, and our cafeteria was Fred Astaire and Ginger Rogers's rehearsal hall.

One day, I have no idea why, Ginger Rogers herself, then in her late sixties but lookin' good, came by the writers' room. We all shook hands, it was very exciting, and after she'd gone, a secretary told me that Ginger had said, referring to me, "He's cute." So, y'know, Howard Hughes can suck it.

While not as attractive as me, the other writers were great. A gag man named Tom Tenowich wrote one of the funniest lines on the show. One week the guest was a blind singer-songwriter and we put into the script some of the real-life things he did, like play golf and skydive. "Whoa," said Mork. "I bet the toughest part is hearing the dog scream on the way down."

Once we got stuck on a line and the room was silent, nothing happening for minutes. Tom, sitting across from the window, suddenly stood up and took a seat on the other side of the room. I was baffled: "Why'd you do that?" Tom leaned in and whispered, "Foiling assassins."

Another time a guy started coughing. "Are you okay?" someone asked. "Yeah, I swallowed a dust ball." "Quick," said Tom, "swallow a maid."

19

Addition by Subtraction

THE THEORIES OF HA!

Since, as of twelve pages ago, we now know there are scientific principles behind humor, it's fair to ask if it has rules. Well, only a fool thinks there are rules to comedy. And only a bigger fool ignores them.

Humor, it's said, is like guerrilla warfare—to succeed you have to travel light, strike unexpectedly, and get away fast.

The principles of professional comedy have grown through trial and error. In Buster Keaton's short "Blacksmith" (1922), he goes about his work while obliviously destroying a beautiful nearby Rolls Royce. Preview audiences hated the bit, and Keaton decided that while people may resent the rich, they admire the beautiful and expensive even more. He reshot the scene with a cheap car and got his laugh.

Keaton was no intellectual, but he knew the importance of understanding how and why gags work, and constructing them precisely. Python members talk about bloody battles over lines; I once almost came to blows with a collaborator over a semicolon in a stage direction. Not something I'm proud of.

Another principle is that the sillier and more absurd the comedy, the more seriously you have to take it. Lewis Carroll wrote logic textbooks; John Cleese says a college course in logic was critical to his career because the crazier the world you create, the clearer its parameters have to be. You can't break a pattern that hasn't been established.

And of course there's timing. On one animated series, I was notorious among the editing staff for adding or cutting a single frame to get the timing just right. A frame is 1/24 of a second.

So here are some rules:

1. Hard consonants (preferably alliterative), like *k* and *p*, and sibilants like *s* are funnier than soft consonants: a **b**oot in the **b**ehind is not as funny as a **kick** in the **p**ant**s**.
2. The number of syllables is important; usually the shorter and punchier the line, the better.
3. Everything's funnier in 3's. Contemporary philosopher Edward de Bono: "The first two variations of a story evoke a pattern in the brain, thus priming it for the punch line, which breaks the pattern."

But that rule (based on pattern recognition) applies to disciplines far beyond comedy—just ask any Delta bluesman or movie murderer.

Logical

In traditional twelve-bar blues, the first two lyric lines are repeated: "Y'know my baby loves me, all you gotta do is see us / Y'know my baby loves me, all you gotta do is see us," followed by a third line with a surprise—"But she asked for a divorce and wants custody of the Prius." ("Divorce Prius Blues" ©2012 Blind Lemon Misch.)

In horror movies, the basic pattern is . . . Attractive, scantily clad young woman enters dark room, looks left (pattern introduced), looks right (pattern established), insane clown with knife leaps from behind (pattern disrupted, along with jugular vein).

And here's a subtler principle, not dissimilar to Steve Martin's theory (pp. 93–94): the best way to get a reaction is to make the audience work, rather than telling it how to feel.

Nothing

In *A Shot in the Dark* (1964), the second original Pink Panther movie, in which Peter Sellers gives one of the great comic performances of all time, Inspector Clouseau is playing billiards with Monsieur Ballon, a murder suspect, when he's called away. Director Blake Edwards heightened Sellers's comedy by contrasting it with Ballon's deadpan reaction . . .

See link 23: Sellers tries to return a pool cue to its rack, with disastrous results, while Ballon stares impassively.

There's a famous noncomedy example in Keaton's *The General* (1926), a scene in which Buster doesn't appear. A Union train is stopped by a burning bridge and the commanding officer makes a decision . . .

See link 24: The officer orders the train forward, the bridge collapses and the train falls into the canyon; the officer watches blankly.

Keaton told the actor to show nothing so the audience would provide the emotion. While you could argue that Keaton's direction was an outgrowth of his own stone-faced persona, it was already a recognized movie technique.

In 1918, Russian filmmaker Lev Kuleshov shot the face of an actor and alternated it with a plate of soup, a woman draped over a coffin, and a little girl with a teddy bear. When the film screened, the audience believed the man was hungry for the soup, sad for the woman, tender about the girl . . . but Kuleshov had used the same shot of the actor each time. It was the audience that did the work, imposing its own changing emotions on an actor who showed nothing.

It's counterintuitive, but sometimes the best way to communicate an emotion—that is, to give something—is to withhold it. Groucho, talking about nudity in movies, said, "It's what you don't see that you're interested in," and that's as true for humor (and drama) as for body parts: to pull people in, leave something out. Addition by subtraction.

In *Police Squad!*, a TV series I wrote with the guys who did *Airplane!*, a key rule was No Mugging; if an actor signaled something was supposed to be funny, we'd lose the laugh.

The ending of the movie *Queen Christina* (1933) has Greta Garbo as a deposed monarch sailing into exile. The actress asked director Rouben Mamoulian what she should think of for the final dramatic shot, which became one of the most powerful moments in screen history. Garbo looks into the distance, thinking of . . . Her lost empire? Her uncertain future?

"Nothing," Mamoulian told her. "Think of nothing."

Sometimes you can increase the response by making 'em wait. In the sitcom *Friends*, one of the main sets was a Manhattan coffee shop,

Nothing

Central Perk. During one show, the ditzy character Phoebe suddenly says, out of nowhere, "*I get it—*Central *Perk!*" Fun gag if it's in the second or third episode; in this case it was season seven.

Whether the laugh goes to you or you to the laugh, comedy also depends on perspective. Psychologist Paul McGhee: "Humor (like beauty) is something that exists only in our minds and not in the real world." Shakespeare agreed, in iambic pentameter: "A jest's prosperity lies in the ear / Of him that hears it, never in the tongue / Of him that makes it."

In other words, what's funny to me might not be to you. (Although in that case you'd be wrong.)

Your degree of sophistication is important too; the more you know about comedy, the more you respond to higher-level humor. But again, that's true of everything—the more you know about any art form, the more discerning your taste.

Still, knowledge and sophistication can make you jaded. Two comedy writers argue about what joke to use in a script: one says, "Number 467"; the other says, "Nah, 119."

20

Heard Any Good Jokes?

George Orwell said, "The aim of a joke is not to degrade the human being but to remind him that he's already degraded." Okay, I feel a lot better.

Freud divided jokes into two types, those with a purpose—to instruct or make a point—and those with no purpose beyond amusement. It's interesting, though, that when he tried to give examples of the latter, he kept finding meanings in them.

Indeed, it's likely there's no joke (just like there's nothing we say or do) that seems to be completely without meaning, because pattern recognition isn't just a human ability but a need.

Broken

When the iPod Nano was first released, owners complained that the "Shuffle" function was broken: their favorite love song kept coming up, four Beatles tunes played in a row, that new Kelly Clarkson track never appeared. In fact, Apple's engineers said the algorithm that generated random plays had been tested and verified repeatedly. The problem wasn't with the iPod but with its owners. Paul Kocher, president of Cryptography Research: "Our brains aren't wired to understand randomness."*

Psychologists use "impossible objects"—drawings like "The Devil's Pitchfork"—to show that the mind's instinctive reaction to an incongruity, a mystery, a puzzle, is to solve it, to resolve it, even if it's unresolvable. There's even an aural equivalent—you hear what sounds like the cry of a person's voice but it's only the rustling of leaves. (Though tragically, it's sometimes the cry of a person being attacked by leaf rustlers.)

Steve Martin was right; humans are compelled to find comedy/order in meaninglessness. Interpreting chaos as order helps us feel safe in a chaotic world and, as a bonus, allows conspiracy theories to thrive and Jesus to appear in tamales.

Brace Yourself

Freud may have been wrong about some jokes being meaningless, but he had a point when he said jokes were intrinsically hostile—they usually make fun of someone or something (similar to what Plato and Aristotle thought on page 45). Monty Python postulated a joke so funny it killed; the British used it against the Nazis, who died laughing.

So it is with great trepidation that I now present to you the actual Funniest Joke in the World.

You remember that a researcher at the University of Wolverhampton found the world's oldest joke (p. 12; ah, but that was long ago, when we were young . . .). In 2002, Richard Wiseman, intriguingly named, of the University of Hertfordshire, set up a website called LaughLab, where people from all over the world could submit and rate jokes, the idea being to find the one that worked for the most people in the most countries. He received forty thousand entries (of which two-thirds were too racist, violent, or dirty to print).

---

* For a prickly, idiosyncratic examination of this subject, see Nassim Nicholas Taleb's *Fooled by Randomness*.

The winner—later discovered to be based on a 1951 sketch written by Spike Milligan for the famed British radio series *The Goon Show*—was submitted by a psychiatrist named Gurpal Gosall, whose name may be funnier than the joke.

Two guys are hunting in the woods when one suddenly falls to the ground, and it looks like he's not breathing. The other guy takes out his cell and calls 911: "My friend is dead. What should I do?" Operator: "Okay, I can help. First we have to make sure he's dead . . ." There's silence, a gunshot, then the guy comes back on the line: "Okay, now what?"

In second place was this:

Sherlock Holmes and Dr. Watson go camping. They pitch their tent under the stars and go to sleep. In the middle of the night, Holmes wakes his friend and says: "Watson, look up at the sky and tell me what you see." Watson: "I see millions and millions of stars." Hol-

mes: "And what do you deduce from that?"

Watson: "Well, if there are millions of stars, and if even a few of those stars have planets, then it's quite likely there are planets like Earth out there. And if there are planets like Earth, there could also be life." Holmes: "No, you idiot, it means someone stole our tent."

Campy

Both of these demonstrate the importance of "precise ambiguity." Take the hunters: *It looks like he's not breathing*—kinda vague, right? But it has to be; the punchline depends on our not knowing if the guy's dead. You have to say it *looks* like he's not breathing because it's what's *not* said that sets up the punchline.

Holmes and Watson also rely on an equivocal phrase: *Look up at the sky and tell me what you see.* For the joke to work, the listener has to either have forgotten the beginning, which had Holmes and Watson *pitching their tent under the stars*; or when Watson says *I see millions of stars,* the listener thinks instantly, subconsciously, "Wait, aren't they in a tent? Oh, David probably just said it wrong, not important, wait, David's still talking, I better listen . . ."

I Killed Roger Ackroyd

Some jokes use specificity rather than ambiguity; i.e., they lie.

> *Guy goes into a doctor's office. Doctor says, "First, you have to stop masturbating. Guy says, "Why?" Doctor says, "So I can examine you."**

Guy goes into a doctor's office—not *Guy goes to a doctor* and especially not *Guy waits in a doctor's office*; the first words have to make you picture a man walking into an office and sitting on a table.

But that makes no sense within the joke: "Guy goes into a doctor's office, doctor says—" So the doctor's already there as the guy walks in and starts masturbating?

The brain never notices. The joke doesn't even bother saying "The doctor comes in," because after you hear the punchline—*So I can examine you*—your mind instantly, subconsciously, goes back and forms a mental picture of a guy masturbating as the doctor enters. (And I'll thank you to keep your dirty mental pictures out of my book.)

It's a twenty-four-word impossible object; either the doctor's waiting for the patient or vice versa—it can't be both. Yet to make the joke's

---

* A friend said, "Put that in the book, you'll have them in the palm of your hand."

illogic work, our brains blithely believe one thing at the beginning and another at the end.

Jokes, mystery stories, and magic tricks all operate by misdirection—keep the audience from the solution by drawing their attention somewhere else. Or by withholding a key piece of information.

In 1926, a young woman named Agatha Christie published a story called "The Murder of Roger Ackroyd," with a plot twist so ingenious that she immediately became the most famous mystery writer in the world.

The secret is in two sentences during a scene where the narrator visits Ackroyd: "The letter was brought in at twenty minutes to nine. It was just on ten minutes to nine when I left him, the letter still unread." What the narrator doesn't say, and what no reader suspects until the end, is that during those ten minutes—spoiler alert—Roger Ackroyd is killed by the narrator.

And he got away with it thanks to the same sneakily precise ambiguity that your Uncle Mel always screws up at parties, especially when he's on his third vodka tonic. (I'm not judging, just being honest.)

Intricate jokes slow the mystery-solution process to the point where you can almost watch your brain return to the beginning and work out the puzzle, what I call a "Brain-Back."

>   *What's the definition of a sadist?*
>   *A person who's kind to a masochist.*

If you're like most people, your brain just went:

>   *Huh?*
>   *Sadist—cruel.*
>   *Masochist—likes pain.*
>   *"A person who's kind to—" Ah . . .*
>   *Ha.*

Best Joke Winner Holmes-and-Watson is a puzzle joke and a Shaggy Dog story—it takes its time, playing with leisurely cosmic conjectures, wending its way toward some important revelation. But what's revealed is what was there all along; you think you're keeping up but you're Wile E. Coyote, already off the cliff, hanging in midair.

In a Shaggy Dog story, the punchline is anticlimactic—the pleasure's in the journey. By that definition, the ultimate Shaggy (or more accurately, Dirty) Dog Story is "The Aristocrats," which became a movie in which different comics tell the same joke over and over for ninety minutes. Considered the dirtiest joke in the world, "The Aristocrats" gets its flavor not from the punchline but from the increasingly elaborate sexual depravity described by whoever's telling it. It's less about dirty than about how long it is and how big it gets.

Wait, that didn't come out right.

One of my favorite dirty jokes is from Sarah Silverman (written by Claudia Lonow): "I was licking jelly off my boyfriend's penis, and I thought . . . I'm becoming my mother." I love that the dirtiness is a cover; the joke is really a parody of clichés about mothers and daughters.

Komedy Kategories

Pretty much any joke fits into a category, but there are too many categories to cover, so I'll hit a few I particularly like.

There's Dumb jokes, which are almost never told that way; after all, it's no fun making fun of stupid people—they're stupid. So Dumb jokes are usually disguised by being about minority groups.

It's an ancient tradition, and your parents' Polish jokes and the Blonde jokes of a few years ago are no different from stories about the dim-witted people of . . . well, whatever country you were in: Schildburg in medieval Germany, Gotam in medieval England. The dunces of the nineteenth-century Polish town of Chelm were popularized by many Jewish writers, including Sholem Aleichem and Nobel Prize–winner Isaac Bashevis Singer.

Being a screenwriter (and part Polish), one of my favorites in the Dumb genre is the Polish actress who wanted to get into the movies so she slept with the screenwriter, which is actually a screenwriter joke, which I'll come back to in a moment.

We add ethnicity or hair color to dumb-person jokes to give them an edge, a little electric current of political incorrectness. But the edges are sharp; you can laugh at this type of joke all you want, and I do, but homogenizing, generalizing, and stereotyping can slide into bigotry.

In the '70s, the magazine *National Lampoon* took that concept to a funny extreme. Tacitly assuming that everyone thinks of Holland as placid and inoffensive, it devoted an article to hating the Dutch, positing the entire country as stupid, lazy, cowardly, venal, and (of course) out to subvert the American way of life. Particularly striking were the racist pamphlets, modeled on Nazi anti-Semitism, which were horrible and hilarious and showed the seductive power of racism.

When the Internet started, entire websites appeared with insulting jokes about particular professions, which broke down into subsets: not just lawyer jokes but malpractice lawyer jokes; not just musician jokes but trumpeter jokes, timpanist jokes. I remember a banjo joke:

Banjo player parks at the mall and leaves his banjo in the back of his car. When he comes back, he's horrified to see that someone broke into his car and left another banjo.

And a psychiatrist joke:

How many Freudians does it take to change a light-bulb? Two—one for the bulb and another to hold the penis I mean ladder.

Show Business Is a Joke

A distinctive characteristic of profession jokes is that they're frequently funny only to the people they're aimed at. I'll illustrate with my own category, show business. First, the actor joke:

> *A producer talks to a studio executive. "You won't believe who I got for our movie—Pitt." "Brad Pitt?!" "Oh, no, Sam Pitt, he's young but great. And guess who's opposite him—Jolie!" "Angelina Jolie?" "No, Mitzi Jolie, the reality star, she's amazing. And guess who else—Gibson!" "Mel Gibson?" "Yes."*

Obviously, the key here is that the teller and tellee know who's currently up and who's down in the movie business.

Here's a producer joke, found funny only by producers:

> *A theater producer's latest play is a box office disaster—only twelve people come to the opening. He meets another producer, who says, "How'd the play go?" First producer: "Not so great. Only fifteen people showed up."*

That's the joke. The reason it's funny to producers is that even with a flop, the producer can't help exaggerating.

The comedian joke:

> *A comic finishes his set and there's a beautiful woman waiting backstage. "That was the most incredible performance I've ever seen," she says. "I am so turned on. Please, take me back to your hotel room and have wet, hot, wild, animal sex with me." And the comic says, "Did you see the first show or the second?"*

The screenwriter joke:

A screenwriter comes home, there's ambulances, fire engines. He finds a cop and says, "What happened?" Cop says, "Your agent came to your house, killed your wife and kids, and burned everything to the ground." Writer: "My agent came to my house?"

One of the Other Puns I Mentioned Earlier

Let's be honest with each other . . . (I, for one, am sick of the deceit): puns are dicey. "Ask for me tomorrow and you shall find me a grave man." C'mon, Will, Mercutio's dying, do we really want wordplay?*

Puns, I feel, require an excuse. One Christmas, a Chicago radio station held a contest for the best joke that had a phrase from a Christmas carol as the punchline:

Two shirts, Phil and Don, are in a clothing store. Phil says, "Don, I'm so excited! Who's gonna buy us? What kinda guy?" Just then a hand comes in, grabs them, and the next thing they know they're in a closet. Soon Phil is taken out and comes back six hours later, a little dirty, a little sweaty. Don: "So what's he like?! Tell me everything!" Phil: "Don, we now are gay apparel.

Some Arbitrary Bests

I canvassed some of my comedy friends and here are two of their favorite jokes:

---

* Joking while in pain reminds me of the story, not a pun, of when Walter Matthau and Jack Lemmon were working on a movie and Matthau fell, hurting his back. Crew members went for a doctor, Lemmon stayed with his pal. "Walter, are you comfortable?" said Lemmon and, through his pain, Matthau answered, "I make a living."

It's the Jewish high holidays, the cantor's singing, when suddenly, over-whelmed by the moment, he drops to his knees, looks heavenward, and cries, "Lord, before you I am nothing!" The rabbi gets swept up too; he falls to his knees and cries to the heavens, "Lord, before you I am nothing!" Mr. Moscowitz, in the seventh row, can't believe his eyes; overwhelmed, he drops to his knees: "Lord, before you I am nothing!" Moscowitz's mother-in-law is sitting a couple rows back with her husband; she turns to him and says, "Get a load of who thinks he's nothing."

Doctor tells a guy, "I have terrible news—you have cancer and Alzheimer's." And the guy says, "Well thank God I don't have cancer."

A psychiatrist once visited my apartment, looked around and said "Hmm, white phone, interesting." Ridiculous, but I guess the things we like, whether phones or jokes, reflect our personalities in *some* way, although the correlation may be obscure.

So I herewith grant you intimate knowledge of my secret life by presenting two of my favorite jokes.

A guy wakes up with a horrible hangover and no wallet—he must have left it at the party. All he remembers is the street and that the house had a golden toilet seat. He drives to the street and picks a house.
    "I'm sorry, I may have been here last night, I'm looking for my wallet, do you have a golden toilet seat?" The door slams in his face. Next house: "I'm sorry, do you have a golden toilet seat?" Door slams in his face. Next house: "Do you have a golden toilet seat?" The woman turns around and yells, "Frank—it's the guy who shit in your tuba."

A Hasidic Jew walks into a bar with a brightly colored tropical parrot on his shoulder. Bartender says, "Whoa, that's amazing, where'd you get it?" Parrot says, "Brooklyn, there's millions of 'em."

21

Love and Theft

PLAGIARISM

All artists begin as plagiarists; if they're successful, theft becomes homage.

That isn't criticism, it's reality. Certainly it's true in the world of comedy, where probably every joke is stolen, even the ones we think we made up. But it's not just jokes; writers say there are only three stories in the world. It's almost certainly true that every idea is a variant on something that came before. Chaucer: "Out of old fields come all the new corn."

But another saying, that we see so far because we stand on the shoulders of giants, loses some force if the giant yells, "Who the hell said you could stand on my shoulders?!"

The question of stealing is big in comedy; after all, material is a comic's blood—remember Berle, the Thief of Bad Gags.

Years ago, I knew a standup whose act consisted of buying a chicken at Albertson's, getting on stage, and goofing with it, making it dance. A

Selfish

famous comedian saw his act, bought a chicken, and went on *The Tonight Show*. The chicken guy threatened to sue, the comic paid him $15,000, but the chicken guy's career was over. Of course, the flip side of the story is that a dancing chicken ain't much to base a career on.

The fact is, stealing is not only constant in the arts but necessary in all areas of life; taking people's ideas and building on them is pretty much the only way new ideas are born. Most true artists, in most circumstances, aren't threatened by it.

During his nightclub days, Woody Allen was told that another comic was doing his jokes. He didn't care—he figured the guy wouldn't do them as well, he wouldn't come up with any more that good, and Woody would.

It's hard to steal from artists who are unique—their styles are too distinctive. When Ron Wood joined the Rolling Stones, he played rhythm guitar along with Keith Richards. After their next album came out, a friend of Wood's listened to a track and said, "Which guitar are you?" Wood answered, "The other one."

The Argentinean fantasist Jorge Luis Borges wrote a short story— "Pierre Monard, Author of The Quixote"—about a man who loves *Don Quixote* so much that he sets out on a quest that is, how shall we put it, quixotic: he decides to write *Don Quixote*. He immerses himself in the world of sixteenth-century Spain, in the culture and language of Cervantes, so that what he writes will be, word for word, the same as *Don Quixote*, yet not a copy but the result of his own imagination.

Stealing works both ways; great artists often use borrowed material. Shakespeare stole almost all his plots. Handel took parts of the *Messiah* from Georg Telemann. Andy Warhol manipulated images made by other people. George Harrison unconsciously copied the '50s hit "He's So Fine" for his '70s hit "My Sweet Lord." The image of Barack Obama in Shepard Fairey's "Hope" poster was an AP photograph.*

You can't own a concept, only the resulting work. No one can copyright the idea of two guys dressing as women to escape gangsters—a good thing, since writers Billy Wilder and I. A. L. Diamond stole the plot of *Some Like It Hot* from a German movie and the title from a Bob Hope movie.**

There are always lawsuits by people who claim they had the idea for the latest hit long before it came out. A popular FedEx commercial last year

Thieves

showed the owner of "AAAAAAAAAAAAAAAAAAAAAA Auto Repair" answering the phone with his company's full name, explaining that it put him first in the phone book. A TV writer then claimed that fifteen years earlier, he had a character who owned "AAAAAAAAAAAAAAAAAAAAAA-1 Plumbers" and announced his arrival at a house with the full name, explaining that it meant he was first in the phone book.

---

* A proponent of "appropriation art," photographer Richard Prince photographs other photographers' photographs.

** Sometimes even the *artist* can't own the work. In Indonesia, a monkey stole a camera then photographed herself; when the photo was published no one knew who to pay, since copyrighted works "must be the product of human authorship."

You gotta feel sorry for the poor schmuck who wrote something for an obscure animated cable show only to see it used years later for a million-dollar ad campaign. Friends urged him to sue, but he knew it would be difficult to win. More important, since the Supreme Court defines corporations as people, he felt that taking a Multinational Person to court using the unlimited resources of a part-time teacher and first-time author was simply unfair.

Condolences for the schmuck may be sent to "Mischy" c/o this publisher.

One of the biggest forces behind strict copyright laws is Mickey Mouse. Until 1975, copyright protection lasted fifty-six years. Then the Walt Disney Co. realized that the first Mickey Mouse short was made in 1928, and the company—whose most famous movies were stolen from stories by European writers stolen from medieval folk tales—spent millions of dollars successfully lobbying Congress to change copyright to 120 years. So if you want to use Mickey for anything, better lawyer up for 2048.

I once tried to sell an updated version of *Cinderella* to Disney, who said they couldn't do a project involving a character from another movie, even if it was their movie.

A few years ago, *Harper's Magazine* published "The Ecstasy of Influence," a lengthy, erudite examination by Jonathan Lethem of the history and issues behind the concepts of originality, appropriation, sampling, copyright, and intellectual property, concluding that all artists build on the work of others and that ideas can't be "stolen." The punchline came at the end, where three pages of small print listed the sources Lethem plagiarized the article from.*

The book *Reality Hunger* by David Shields consists of acknowledged but unattributed quotes by other people—Shields didn't write

---

* This chapter's title is plagiarized from an album by Bob Dylan, who's been accused of plagiarizing melodies, lyrics, prose, and pictures.

a word. Teenage German novelist Helene Hegemann, accused of plagiarism, said, "There's no such thing as originality, just authenticity."

Originality isn't about the concept but about how that concept is expressed. The task of artists is to grab something from the infinite churn of ideas—whether it's someone else's idea or not—then express it in a way unique to that artist.

In *The Simpsons*, a TV producer is accused of plagiarism and says, "You take away our right to steal ideas, where are they gonna come from?"

22

Saying It Worse

THE PHILOSOPHY OF HA!

Stolen or not, a joke is valuable only if it works. So can anyone explain how comedy works? Robert Frost was asked to explain one of his poems and answered, "You mean you want me to say it worse?"

Most of the great philosophers took a whack at defining humor. Thomas Hobbes said it's a mean-spirited way of proving your superiority. (Laughter at yourself is explained as scorning your weaknesses, but Superiority Theory really has no explanation for nonsense, wordplay, or surprise.) Immanuel Kant was less judgmental; his Incongruity Theory says, "Laughter is an effect that arises if a tense expectation is transformed into nothing." (Essentially what the evolutionary biologists said on pages 87–88.) Schopenhauer had a theory similar to Kant's but I don't have an opinion about it; I just like mentioning Schopenhauer because it makes me seem more intelligent.

Herbert Spencer adjusted Kant's theory into Descending Incongruity—humor comes when "the conscious is transferred from great things to small" (Woody Allen's "I don't believe in an afterlife, although I am bringing a change of underwear," page 80). Author Arthur Koestler said humor is the result of two different frames of reference colliding,* what Freud called "the coupling of dissimilar things to bring forth what's hidden."

To show the subject's complexity, contemporary philosopher John Morreall declares comedy comes from a "cognitive shift" at the moment of Koestler's Kollision, while Robert Latta says it can happen after, when you recognize the "solution" to an incongruity (in a joke, the punchline); or before, when you realize something funny's coming and laugh before it happens (a phenomenon known as premature ejokeulation).

Let John and Bob argue timing—we've now heard from philosophers, doctors, neuroscientists, psychiatrists, psychologists, biologists, anthropologists, novelists, historians, British people, Jews, and even an occasional comedian. Although we await the views of hockey players, surely we've tracked our prey to its lair; somewhere in the charged flux of violated expectations, incongruous juxtapositions, and abrupt perspective-shift, Humor waits, ready to fling its pie.

I'm gonna call it: Rapid Juxtaposition of Dissimilar Concepts describes anything funny—verbal, physical, or visual.

Which means . . . we've done it. We've defined humor. Hooray! Champagne and hookers for everyone! (I'll wait while you finish.)

Oh, hold on, there's a problem—our definition describes comedy but not *just* comedy. Which is the problem for all humor-definers. Kant's Incongruity Theory applies to pretty much any art form; tension and resolution is the underpinning of prose, poetry, painting, sculpture, music, and every horror movie ever made.

Worse, the theory fails on the level of day-to-day living; if Kant and the evolutionary biologists were right, there'd be no such thing as "Phew"—every time a danger passed, we'd be in hysterics.

Or take physical comedy—Rapid Juxtaposition of Dissimilar Concepts describes someone who's vertical rapidly becoming

---

* Koestler told what is, in my opinion, the best political theory joke of all time (a category that, I admit, is not large): "Capitalism is the exploitation of man by man, while Communism is the reverse."

horizontal; or as one less learned than I might say it, falling down. But the same description applies to someone who's been shot, which is sometimes not funny.

Just as there's no principle of comedy that doesn't apply to drama, even the most rarified definition of art works just as well for cheap yucks. For instance, my fellow English majors (i.e., the unemployed) know that juxtaposition of contrasting images is the foundation of metaphor. Poet Octavio Paz:

Funny?

"The poetic image is an embrace of opposite realities." Well, Jim Carrey and a rhinoceros's butt are different realities. So does the former coming out of the latter mean that *Ace Ventura: When Nature Calls* is poetry?

It certainly seems like Freud's "coupling of dissimilar things," which is a version of *cognitive dissonance*, the psychological condition of holding two opposing ideas simultaneously. The recognized response to that is rationalization; yet when presented with a large African mammal apparently excreting an American movie star, the brain just accepts it as pleasingly ridiculous. Why that happens instead of the brain exploding in a hideous flood of short-circuited synapses and rancid cranial fluid, no one knows.

Popular Mechanics

Since there's no clear explanation for why humans find things funny, let's examine one type of humor, physical comedy, and try to explain that.

French philosopher Henri Bergson believed comedy involves making fun of either the animalistic or mechanical aspects of human nature. Mechanical is the habits or patterns we have trouble changing, like an American driving on the right side in England. For Bergson, people who are inflexible and act like a machine (or objects that seem as if they're alive) aren't just interesting or surprising—they're funny.

Think of the gag of a newscaster mindlessly reading ridiculous things from a teleprompter, or Charlie Chaplin caught in the gears of a machine—essentially becoming part machine himself— then when he comes out, acting like a robot, using his pliers to tighten anything with knobs, including the buttons on a woman's dress (*Modern Times*, 1932).

Silent comedy, being almost entirely physical, provides endless examples of mechanical humor. Critic Walter Kerr, in *The Silent Clowns* (a gorgeous coffee table book with brilliant analyses of Keaton, Chaplin, and Harold Lloyd, now sadly out of print but available in libraries and on the net), notes that the obstacles in Keaton's films are less often people than elements of nature—wind, rocks, water. Keaton triumphs when he stops fighting and instead merges with them or an object.

The Balloonatic (1923) provides two wonderful examples. Buster's on top of a hot-air balloon when it unexpectedly takes off; then he's lost in the wilderness, making a meal in a canoe . . .

See link 25: Aloft atop a balloon, Keaton climbs down and drops into the basket—but the bottom falls out. Keaton hangs on, his head obscured, legs sticking out below, so that the balloon looks like a giant head above tiny legs. Then, in a canoe, Buster burns out the bottom and is later seen floating down the river. Spotting a rabbit, he takes out a rifle and stands to shoot . . . he was walking through shallow water with the canoe wedged around him.

Kerr points out how Keaton merges with the balloon and canoe in what Bergson called "the mechanical encrusted on the living"— Keaton becomes half-man, half-object. (The melding of human and object is also a key element of Cubism.)

As for people acting like animals, think of all the comedy based on animalistic functions like sex, eating, going to the bathroom—though hopefully not all three at once. (Some people object to being likened to animals, but the alternatives, Hugh Hefner points out, are vegetables and minerals.) The more you look for it, the interrelationship of humans, animals, and machines seems to be at the crux of comedy.

Is the Penis a Phallic Symbol?

Freud saw more animal than mechanical in people and thought humor was a form of primitive (animal) aggression. He also said comedians made a religion of childishness.* Indeed, children (like Trickster) say and do things forbidden to adults, and are fascinated by the four comedy food-groups: verbal aggression, body functions, sex, and violence.

Freud also viewed humor as an expression of male sexuality, noting the canes and cigars used by so many comics. One wonders how he'd react to the male frontal nudity in contemporary movies. Although sometimes a penis is only a penis.**

Yet despite thinking it was childish and sexually aggressive, Freud said comedy is crucial to humanity. He believed jokes happen when the conscious mind allows in—and out—thoughts and urges that are usually repressed (Relief Theory).

Freud agreed with Plato, who complained that "comedy invites the soul to indulge in desires," except that Freud thought that was a *good* thing; expressing suppressions releases tension and "psychic energy." Humor is therapeutic, like sleep and dreams, a coping mechanism for stressful situations, similar to neuroses or even delusions

---

* Children, living in a presocialized state, are often seen as primitive or animalistic. Especially if they're told they can't have more gummi bears because, come on, lunch is in a couple hours and you just had crackers. But I digress.
** While cigars may be phallic symbols, comics also use them for timing: say the line then puff till the laugh ends.

but healthier. This explains why humor exists in even the most difficult circumstances.

In Soviet Russia, where there were constant food shortages, they told this joke: A woman goes into a butcher shop and asks, "Do you have any fish?" Butcher: "No, here we don't have meat. Fish they don't have across the street."

23

When Did You Break Your Collarbone?

BUSTER KEATON

I've brought Keaton up a few times—he's an idol of mine. Chaplin was and is more popular, but deciding between them is like John vs. Paul; they're both great, so who you like says as much about you as them. I love Chaplin—*City Lights*, *The Gold Rush*, and some of the shorts are works of genius. But I find Keaton more provocative, more mysterious, more profound, more modern.

The legend goes that in 1896, Joseph Frank Keaton was backstage at a medicine show run by his father with magician Harry Houdini, when he fell down a flight of stairs. Seeing Keaton wasn't hurt, Houdini said, "That sure was a buster," meaning a rough fall, giving Keaton both a life-long nickname and a vocation. He was six months old.

Of course, he wasn't performing slapstick comedy with his parents at the age of six months, that would be ridiculous—he didn't join the act till he was three. As the Human Mop, he got thrown around the stage, kicked in the face, and hit so much that his father was repeatedly arrested for child abuse, though it was

Nihilist

all part of the act, and Buster said he never minded and in seventeen years never got hurt.

Keaton told a story (probably apocryphal, but hey, it's his story) that when he was a toddler, a cyclone sucked him out of his bedroom and set him down four blocks away unharmed. It doesn't matter if it's true because it goes to the heart of Keaton as an artist: the arc described by his body in space.

That's another insight of Walter Kerr in *The Silent Clowns* (p. 136). He talks about Keaton's relationship to Nature—the Keaton Curve as he flies through the air, propelled by ladders, trees, cars, and occasionally, gravity. The way Keaton used his body became a touchstone for performers as disparate as Johnny Depp and Jackie Chan.

In the short "Neighbors" (1920), Keaton zips across a yard on a pulley through a window into a building, slides down two flights on a banister, then out another window and across the yard again on a clothesline.

His most famous stunt ("gag") was in *Steamboat Bill Jr.* (1928). In the middle of a hurricane, Keaton gets knocked to the ground then stands up, dazed. As he rubs his neck, the front of a house crashes down on him, his body miraculously passing through a small window at the top.

For that gag there were five jet engines at the side of the set providing the hurricane. Because of the wind, the façade had to be heavy enough not to bend or twist while falling—it weighed two tons. The clearance around Keaton's head and shoulders totaled three inches.

The cameraman assumed Keaton would be killed and refused to film; he set up the shot and walked away, leaving Keaton to turn on the camera himself...

See link 26: Keaton miraculously avoids death by house-squash.

Another time, Keaton speeds on a motorcycle along an elevated railroad trestle, not knowing there's a huge gap in the tracks ahead. Keaton keeps going, then two trucks enter the gap from opposite directions, their roofs together the exact width and height of the gap, and Keaton drives right over them.

That gag's one of many where Keaton survives by not opposing but accepting the forces of Nature. Kerr notes that "as treacherous as the universe might be, Keaton always trusted it."

Keaton loved machines and objects but only for what they could do. When Chaplin makes something out of something else—dancing feet out of potatoes in *The Gold Rush*—it's playful; for Keaton, it's practical.

In a chase, he drives his convertible into a lake . . . then raises the roof so it becomes a sail-car.

Stone

Keaton was famous for never smiling. The Great Stone Face was the anti-Chaplin, rejecting even a hint of pathos, not asking for sympathy or even laughs: "Never beg," he said. Yet without words, without even expression, he somehow conveyed universal humanity.

Unlike Chaplin and Lloyd, Keaton's persona developed from no worked-out principle or theory of comedy. Again, he was practical: "I noticed that whenever I smiled, the audience didn't laugh as much." Because we're not told how to feel, Keaton's reactions are a mystery we need to solve, so we project our feelings onto him (like in Kuleshov's experiment on page 113).

Keaton acted with his body. He was short, which helped him pretend to be weak, but he was a real athlete. In *College* (1927), he tries to impress a girl by doing various sports, failing miserably at each. Then at the end, he races across campus, rowing, jumping hurdles, and pole-vaulting to save her. With the exception of the final stunt, where he was doubled by an Olympic pole-vaulter, it's all Keaton.

In his sixty-year career Keaton was doubled one other time, but he didn't know it. Richard Lester, the Beatles director, cast him in *A*

Funny Thing Happened on the Way to the Forum (1966), in a small role that consisted mostly of running.

In one scene Keaton was supposed to bash into a thick tree branch and get knocked down. Lester knew the actor was dying of cancer, so without telling Keaton, he used a stunt man for the shot. Later, an assistant found Lester in his trailer crying, saying "I just got a stunt man for Buster Keaton."

How tough was Keaton? One gag had him falling onto some railroad tracks. His head hit a rail, giving him a headache; he took the afternoon off then came back the next day. Ten years later Keaton got an X-ray for a routine physical and the doctor asked, "When did you break your collarbone?"

In addition to his physical gifts and comic genius, Keaton was one of film's great innovators. His first job in movies was with the clown and director Fatty Arbuckle's company and the first thing he did was ask to bring the camera home, where he took it apart and put it together again to see how it worked. He codirected many of his movies and was as enthusiastic about special effects as he was about intricately worked-out gags.

Before he shot "The Playhouse" (1921), Keaton broke his ankle. His solution to not being able to walk but needing to keep the movie moving was to have his character dream of a theater filled with himself—everyone on stage, in the orchestra pit, and in the audience is Keaton, in multiple exposures showing up to eight of him simultaneously. Each of those shots required mathematical precision, using technology incredibly more primitive than today's.

Surreality Show

Though hardly a theoretician, Keaton was instinctively perceptive about the medium of film; he used its one-dimensionality, its rectangular frame, and even its essential nature—the way it pretends to reality—to unprecedented comic effect. His fascination with movies as an alternative reality reached its height in 1924's *Sherlock, Jr.*, which some people feel is the closest America's come to an actual surrealist film.

Its most famous bit, where Keaton's a projectionist whose spirit walks into the movie he's showing, has been copied by everyone from Woody Allen* to Arnold Schwarzenegger, and again, the technology it required was so complex that it's only a few years ago that people figured out how he did it. (Here I should probably tell you how he did it, but I've read the explanation and I still have no idea.)

Inside the movie, whenever the background changes, Buster's forced to adapt; he's in the middle of traffic dodging cars, then next to a tiger in the jungle, then on a reef in the middle of the ocean. He dives off a rock and gets stuck in a snowbank . . .

See link 27: Keaton walks into a movie.

Keaton was going for laughs, but the sequence draws gasps. It's almost more dream than comedy (though Freud said the two are related on page 137). And once again, Keaton merges with rather than opposes the obstacles he faces. Just like with his relationship to Nature, Keaton's both a part of the movie yet apart. Comedians, like Trickster, are by definition outsiders, in society yet standing outside commenting on it.

Another astonishing gag used no special effects: Keaton's chased by thugs and runs into an alley, where a lady peddler with a tray gestures for him to jump . . . into the tray. Keaton leaps in and disappears. The peddler then walks away as the baffled thugs search for Keaton.

It was one of Keaton's old vaudeville tricks—the peddler's in front of a fence hiding a trap door, her legs held over the door by a horizontal board hidden under her skirt, weighted to hide Buster as he dives through . . .

---

* Allen *really* liked the concept: entering a movie was the central conceit of his film *The Purple Rose of Cairo*, entering a book was the idea of his short story "The Kugelmass Episode" (p. 89), and in *Annie Hall* (starring Woody's girlfriend at the time, an actress named Keaton), Annie's spirit gets up during sex to watch from a chair.

See link 28: Keaton leaps through a person.

In another "Sherlock" gag imported from vaudeville, Keaton needs to escape from bad guys and jumps through a window where he'd earlier put a flat circular box, coming out the other side dressed as a woman—the costume was hidden, perfectly positioned, inside the box. As the magicians Penn & Teller showed, knowing how the trick's done makes it even more amazing . . .

See link 29: Keaton becomes a woman in midair.

Rocks

One of my favorite Keaton visual gags is when a wealthy Buster decides to visit his girlfriend. He gets into his expensive, chauffeured car; the car pulls away, makes a U-turn, stops, and Keaton gets out; the girl lives across the street, but he had to be driven there.

A series of stunts in *Seven Chances* (1925) rank with the house-fall as some of the most amazing in film comedy. *Chances* was adapted from a Broadway play, and it shows—the first two-thirds of the picture is static and, frankly, boring. But it's all setup.

Keaton's a rich playboy, and his fed-up father says he has one week to get married or he'll be cut out of the will. Keaton tries a different girl each day, but it goes badly, and on Saturday he puts an ad in the paper: "Millionaire wants wife. If interested, go to the church at noon Sunday."

Keaton arrives early and falls asleep. In one of the more incredible images in American film, he wakes up surrounded by hundreds of women in bridal gowns.

Meanwhile, the girl he loves says yes, but he has to get to her by seven o'clock. He runs off, and the brides chase him through town and into the desert. (Walter Kerr described Keaton running with "the joy of an arrow going straight" and observed that his seeming stillness in motion is a metaphor for movies themselves, which are, after all, a series of individual still photographs.)

After the picture was finished, Keaton had a preview and noticed the audience laugh when he ran down a hill and accidentally knocked over some rocks, which seemed to follow after him. So he reshot the scene as if the rocks are attacking . . .

See link 30: Keaton escapes from brides only to be pursued by rocks.

Most of that scene shows a small man hurtling through a large landscape. Keaton was all about scale. He always used long-shots for his most elaborate physical gags, believing his body was funniest when seen in relationship to the world. Charlie Chaplin said, "Life is a tragedy in close-up and a comedy in long-shot"; that small figure in the distance—falling, rolling, bouncing—is funny, but up close we'd see the grimace of pain, the physical toll on the fragile flesh.

Those of us who believe in Keaton's genius see both the comic and tragic in his films. While Keaton always denied any intellectual pretense (asked about deeper meanings, he said, "I don't feel qualified to talk about my work"), he knew he was shooting for something beyond slapstick; he hired dramatic directors to keep his movies grounded and reshot their footage when he found it unconvincing.

Keaton's sensibility becomes philosophical when you see a lone man dodging an endless series of rocks, a nihilist's perfect metaphor for existence.

The Saddest Smile

The real Great Stone Face was far from impassive—offscreen, Keaton laughed easily and often. But his life was a roller coaster with emotions he never showed in his movies. He went from the height of fame with a spectacular Beverly Hills Roman Villa mansion to a disastrous marriage, heavy drinking, and the loss of his career, children, and fortune within the span of a couple years.

In 1934, an alcoholic without a movie contract, Keaton did a cheap French film. Perhaps sensing that he was entering a terrible wilderness, at the end, right before he kisses the girl, the Great Stone Face turns to the camera and, for only time in his career, smiles—maybe the saddest smile in the world.

For the next twenty years Keaton worked as a lowly gag writer at MGM, where he'd been one of the highest-paid movie stars in the world. But he never complained, and he gave his great bits to countless comics; taking everything wooden off a moving train and burning it to fuel the engine, from *The General*, became the end of a Marx Brothers movie.*

A gag Keaton devised for comedian Red Skelton comes right out of Trickster mythology. A story about the Nigerian Trickster Edshu (p. 10) has him wearing a hat that's red on one side and blue on the other so people will argue about its color. (What can I say, practical jokes were different in mythological times.)

In *A Southern Yankee*, Skelton's trapped in a Civil War battlefield. To escape, he quickly stitches a flag that's Union on one side and Confederate on the other, then walks through the battle as soldiers on both sides stop shooting and salute . . . till a gust of wind blows the flag around and they resume shooting.

Even today, filmmakers keep taking from Keaton. The bride chase was in a misbegotten remake of *Seven Chances* called *The Bachelor* (1999), with Chris O'Donnell. More happily, Peter Bogdanovich—an expert on film history—adapted the same bit in his 1972 tribute to screwball comedy, *What's Up, Doc*, with Barbra Streisand and Ryan O'Neal accidentally knocking over garbage cans that chase a pedestrian down a San Francisco hill. Director Andrew Stanton used Keaton's face as an inspiration for *Wall-E* (2008) and had his hero pursued by a horde of runaway shopping carts. ** Baz Luhrmann's epic flop *Australia* (2008) ended with a cattle drive through the middle of a town, first done by Keaton in *Go West* (1925). And the *Steamboat Bill Jr.* house-drop has

---

* They did *not* do his stunt of having an entire train fall into a canyon (p. 113), the single most expensive shot of the silent film era.
** Even Keaton stole from Keaton, substituting barrels for rocks in his *own* remake of the gag.

been in everything from "Weird Al" Yankovic videos to *The Simpsons* to *Jackass*.

He Kept Walking

The last thirty years of Keaton's life could be seen as the literalization of one of his stunts: a long, terrifying fall from which he emerged, incredibly, happy and safe. He quit drinking and slowly worked his way back; in the '50s, he was rediscovered through television and even got his own series. He was asked if it was true that in his first movie with Arbuckle in 1917, he lifted one leg onto a counter then the other without immediately falling over; to prove it, Keaton did it right then . . . at the age of sixty-two.

Now happily married, in 1965 Keaton traveled to Italy to see *The General* at the Venice Film Festival, where it—and he—got a ten-minute standing ovation. A few months later, Buster had a seizure; he couldn't recognize anyone, he didn't know who he was . . . but his wife reported that his body, that incredible body that nothing could stop, kept walking around by itself for hours.

The General and Chaplin's *The Gold Rush* are considered the greatest silent comedies and both are usually listed in the Top 10 of best films ever. When my daughter was little, I took her to *The General* at the Silent Movie Theater in Hollywood and saw some of the top comedy writers in the business with their kids.

Some have said that Buster Keaton is the quintessential American comic figure. But I'd go further. The pluck, the gumption, the inventiveness, the stoic self-reliance, the endless energy, the optimism, the refusal to quit and eagerness to fight when necessary, the buoyant romanticism—to an acolyte like me, Buster Keaton *is* America, America at its best.

And man, could that guy end movies.

In *Sherlock, Jr.*, Keaton, the shy innocent, watches a romantic movie with his girl. The debonair movie hero takes his girl's hands; so does

Keaton. The hero gives her a ring; so does Keaton. The hero kisses her; so does Keaton. Then the movie scene dissolves to the hero and his girl with three babies; Keaton scratches his head.

In *Steamboat Bill Jr.*, a flood's ravaged the town. After saving his girl and her father, Keaton proposes. She points out there's no minister . . . and Keaton leaps into the water. She—and we—are baffled . . . then moments later Keaton swims back, pulling a soggy priest.

In *College*, after more than an hour of trying to get the girl, the ending is twenty-four seconds long. The happy couple runs into a church: dissolve to them coming out married; dissolve to them in a house playing with their kids; dissolve to them middle aged, him smoking a pipe, her reading; dissolve to two gravestones and the words THE END.

24

Kosmik Komedy

THE PURPOSE OF HA!

Comedy is obviously different from drama. Obviously.

But, er ... how? After all, a great man once said there is no principle of comedy that doesn't also apply to drama.*

Husband brings boss home for dinner, wife burns a roast—funny if Lucille Ball does it in a sitcom, but in a drama about a couple in a desperate financial situation, it's tragedy. I once had the idea of mimicking a sitcom laugh track by doing a dramatic scene with a "moan track." (I tried to copyright this idea, but there was a prior claim, by a Mr. Aeschylus, filed in 498 BC under the far inferior title "Greek chorus.")

Tragic

In a TV show I had a scene where a woman, furious that a man doesn't love her, tears through a room, destroying everything. After the actress's first take, the producer was blown away: "That was amazing," he said. "She really nailed it, she was so emotional." But the actress was miserable—she knew she'd done it emotionally but not funny. The same words, the same actions, could be played either way.

---

* Misch: *Funny: The Book*, p. 2. (Wow, I just thought of that theory and it already has a citation!)

"Everything is defined by its opposite," says graphic designer Milton Glaser. But drama and comedy are less opposite than two sides of the same artistic coin. If we accept MAP (the Miserable Actress Postulate), it's all about attitude: my TV scene could have been tragic—a sweet woman undone by infatuation with a feckless lover; or comedic—a silly girl throwing a childish tantrum, all depending on how she played it.

So comedy and drama are different yet complementary. Still, many people denigrate comedy; Woody Allen complained that critics treat comics like they're sitting at the children's table. But comedy requires as much skill as drama and can be just as challenging for its audience. I'll put what I've learned from Keaton and Python against Kant and Plato any day. (That I know practically nothing about Kant or Plato seems to me beside the point.)

Must comedy sit with the kiddies for another twenty-four hundred years, or can we finally admit it's an art form? Maybe the question is less about what comedy is than what it makes: laughter. Both laughter and tears spring from overwhelming emotion, yet the causes of laughter—wordplay, funny faces, fat guys falling—seem less dignified than the reasons we cry: sadness, longing, despair.

Maybe the noise is the problem. If we laughed in despair and sobbed in delight, would comedy get more respect?

There seems to be a general belief that drama touches something deep inside us while comedy is usually trivial. But what's the basis for that? The greatest artists admire both: Shakespeare, Picasso, Mozart all mix comedy and drama freely in their masterpieces.

Maybe it's not the artists but the audience that's prejudiced against taking something light and funny "too seriously" or something serious "too lightly." This opus proudly champions the former—Take Funny Seriously!—and every self-help book urges the latter: overcome adversity by maintaining a light (positive, happy, optimistic) attitude.

Because even if comedy provided nothing but laughter, since when is joy a second-string emotion? Jung said Trickster is among the central archetypes of the human identity, so humor isn't just frivolous japery. Or, more precisely, it's *important* frivolous japery.

Contrary to what the anthropologists thought (p. 88), or Freud (p. 137), comedy isn't the mere release of personal or societal tension—it's an active source of the emotional fuel humanity needs to do more than just survive, what author Philip Pullman calls "the value of simple delight."

Comedy vs. Humanity

Unfortunately, reality is a buzzkill. Buddha asked, "How can there be mirth or laughter when the world is on fire?" And Billy Joel was wrong—we started the fire, some would say with that snuck snack in Eden.

We're no angels and we know it; with wacky shenanigans like racism, poverty, war, and environmental devastation, it's like Mark Twain said: "Man is the only animal who blushes, or needs to."

Human imperfection. That's what critic Louis Kronenberger believes is the true subject of comedy: our failure to live up to our ideals. Nineteenth-century writer William Hazlitt: "Only Man is struck with the difference between what things are and what they should be." Groucho: "Those are my principles. And if you don't like them, I have others."

Traditionally, tragedy is about heroes undone by terrible flaws. Comedy doesn't believe in heroes; it's about foolish people—all of us—acting foolishly.

Tragedy says humans could be great if they weren't weak, which is sad. Comedy says humans are weak but think they could be great, which is funny.

Or, to put it more pretentiously:

Tragedy is idealistic—it believes in human perfectibility
but shows how we fall short.
Comedy is skeptical—it believes our fallen state is
predetermined, and deserved.
Tragedy laments human flaws; comedy mocks them but,
in mocking, accepts them.

Comedy vs. the Universe

Remember that Trickster's realm was satirizing not just our foolishness but our hopeless attempts to understand a universe that doesn't seem to know we exist. When we think about humor revealing our intrinsically corrupt natures and complete irrelevance to a senseless, destructive cosmos, we can understand H. L. Mencken: "God is a comedian, playing to an audience too afraid to laugh."

God made us flawed and put us in a world filled with misery and pain, and instead of laughing at the absurdity or crying at the injustice, we worship him. Maybe that's funny to Him: a Ferlinghetti poem describes "the music of the spheres [as] some kind of mad mad laughter."

Our laughter can be bitter, but it's one way to deal with the bleakness of life, along with religion and malt liquor. Lord Byron: "And if I laugh at any mortal thing / 'Tis that I may not weep." Groucho: "If I hadn't known sadness, I wouldn't have spent so much time trying to make people laugh."

If you don't think the bleakness of life can be funny, talk to Vladimir and Estragon in *Waiting for Godot* (Beckett got the name Godot from a Keaton movie). Or Laurel and Hardy—actor Michael McKean points out that all their films are about them failing: "We know they're doomed, and that's why we're laughing."

Is that what's at the heart of comedy? That we know *we're* doomed and that's why we're laughing?

If that's true, how does comedy make anything better? Is Mel Brooks right? If comedy is you falling into a sewer, does that mean

Funny

that (other people's) suffering is funny? When we see Ben Stiller in yet another disaster with his wife's parents, are we cruel to laugh?

No. We relive, and relieve, the delightful horror, the agonizing hilarity of being in a similar fix. "Someday," the saying goes, "we'll look back on this and laugh." Or in comedian Steve Allen's formulation, Comedy = Tragedy + Time.*

And sometimes we subtract the Time. Playwright Sarah Ruhl: "Lightness isn't stupidity. It's a philosophical and aesthetic viewpoint, deeply serious, and has a kind of wisdom—stepping back to laugh at horrible things even as you experience them."

To laugh at suffering is an act of exorcism, expelling the trauma from the horrible thing that has happened, is happening, or could happen to us. Comedy reminds us that life is pain, but pain is surmountable.

And that for the moment, it's Ben Stiller, not me.

---

* Phil Austin of the comedy group Firesign Theatre has an existential variant in his recipe for dead rabbit, the ingredients for which are time and a rabbit.

25

Suffering Is Funny

THE OFFICE

Case in point: *The Office*, a sitcom about workers suffering a boss, Michael Scott, who is simultaneously smug and insecure, patronizing and sycophantic, and who himself suffers as much or more than any of them. (Steve Carell, who played Michael, left the show in 2011; this chapter focuses on the years when he was the star.)

What's remarkable about this multifaceted sitcom is how not just Michael but every character in the large cast can be admirable, hor-

rible, witty, stupid, skilled, and incompetent all at once, defying the rule that on sitcoms, people are defined by a single characteristic (like medicine's mythical "humours," page 49).

The advantage of single-trait, predictable characters is that when *All in the Family*'s racist Archie Bunker got stuck in an elevator with a pregnant black woman, the audience laughed before

Suffering

either said a word; the situation, based on the character, made the comedy. In sitcoms, the situation changes but not the character. When you know the character, the fun comes from his or her predictable reaction to a new situation.

The complexity of *The Office*'s characters means that at any given moment, you *don't* know how they'll react—you don't even know if the moment will be comedy or drama.

The show isn't perfect. I thought it started tentatively, while in later years, it's focused on major plot developments that seem to run counter to its strength: showing the small moments and emotions that are often the most important things in our lives.

But overall, I'm in awe of the whole enterprise. The writing's brilliant, the production flawless (especially since I thought the whole mockumentary* convention played out before the show went on the air). And the acting . . . Watch an old *All in the Family*, or a Sheen-era *Two and a Half Men*; Carroll O'Connor/Charlie Sheen says something outrageous, then sets his expression—defiant, horrified, pleading—while the audience's laughter rolls over his frozen face. It's less acting than posturing.

In *The Office*, thanks partially to the format and partially to the cast, the acting, as well as the dialogue, is filled with subtleties and subtext. Subtext! In a sitcom!

Credit for a lot of this goes to the show's provenance. Ricky Gervais and Stephen Merchant's British *Office* has the same setup, the boss is obnoxious in similar ways, and many of the characters are counterparts of the American ones. But there's a small, critical shift in two major areas: tone and star. Gervais modeled David Brent on a horrific boss he had and it's clear that revenge is the character's genesis. For

---

* Starting with *I Love Lucy* in 1951, sitcoms were videotaped in front of live audiences. TV mockumentaries (the term was invented for the metal-music parody *This Is Spinal Tap*) film with a handheld camera and no audience; the effect is of a weekly short independent movie.

the bulk of the short British series, Brent's only non-negative qualities were his pathetic neediness and loneliness.

Some people resisted that *Office*, finding the relentless humiliations of Brent too squirm-inducing to watch. (In a way, the American David Brent is really Larry David on *Curb Your Enthusiasm*: almost irredeemably offensive, entitled, and narcissistic—we watch aghast/delighted as he furiously digs himself into bottomless chasms of disaster.)

Near the end of the British series, Brent meets a girl who inexplicably "gets" him—which means she's seriously screwed up herself—but it was nice that Brent had a shot at redemption; given the chance to be his usual sexist, insensitive self, he actually stands up for the woman he loves.

Still, for the most part, the British *Office* existed to make fun of the boss. In the American version (adapted by Gervais and Merchant with *Simpsons* writer Greg Daniels), Michael is equally obnoxious and gets humiliated just as often, but we see a basic decency struggling to get past his loneliness-induced aggression, and occasionally that decency comes out, though never in a simplistically redemptive "They-can-do-drama-too!" kinda way.

The tone, reflected primarily in the show's attitude towards Michael, isn't condescending. Rather than simply laughing at him, we're asked to look at his miserable behavior and, in recognizing its source, root for him to overcome his nature.

You could see *The Office* as the ultimate Liberal sitcom: it says that bad behavior often comes from bad circumstances; that people are basically good—deeply flawed, but capable of growth if given dignity and respect.

The Groin of the Face

All its characters are drawn with humanity. Take Dwight K. Schrute. Every sitcom has its fool, a clown, someone to either make fun of or be the enemy. One template is Lucille Ball's boss Mr. Mooney in *Here's*

Lucy—a laughable, stuffy, officious male dowager who exists only to be frustrated by Lucy's zany antics. Even a show as sophisticated as *M*A*S*H* fell into the trap with the boob Frank Burns.

But in the same way that *M*A*S*H* stepped up by replacing Burns with the stuffy but smart Charles Winchester, *The Office* quickly gave Dwight positive characteristics: though ruthless and rigid and smug and superior, he saw the receptionist Pam crying in a stairwell, came over and hugged her. And the tiny flinch she gave as he approached made the moment even sweeter.

In a sense, Dwight is *The Office's* Trickster: the outrageous upender of social conventions. Yet even his foolishness is different from the usual sitcom clowns, since it comes from a not entirely unearned cockiness, like with his martial arts expertise. (Talking about attacking his opponent's head, he sagely observes, "The eyes are the groin of the face.")

Pam's husband Jim is a weaker character, but even he's drawn in consistently surprising ways. It was clear from the beginning that he's underemployed—he's smart, funny, good at his job. But Dwight, and even Michael, can be more effective salesmen, and we've seen Jim thrust into leadership and flounder.

It's a real ensemble but Steve Carell was first among equals; his performance, being consistently offensive while allowing us to see his inner despair, without asking for our pity, was a quiet tour de force. Here is a character that presents as cardboard but is actually filled with depth.

In one episode, Michael reads from a suggestion box to impress his boss from corporate headquarters, who he'd slept with. Carell shows Michael going from pompous condescension to increasingly desperate hostility as the situation slips out of his control . . .

See link 31: Michael reads suggestions that range from "doing something about your morning breath" to asking "why you boned your boss."

Carell takes lines that scream "insensitive moron" and makes them unexploitedly funny. Trying to convince black salesman Stanley not to leave for a higher-paying job he says, "Mo' money, mo' problems—you of all people should know that."

Racist, unconscionable—but the way Carell underplays the line, almost muttered, lets you see that beneath Michael's desperate grab at a demeaning racial trope to make a connection, there's resentment and pain at the possibility of losing a man who is, like everyone at the office, someone he lovingly, and totally inaccurately, considers a close friend.

When Michael has to fire an employee on Halloween, Carell and Jenna Fischer, as Pam, show the shift in power between them based on who needs what from whom . . .

See link 32: Wearing a ludicrous "two-headed" costume, Michael tells Pam he's going to fire someone and asks "who you think it will be, based on job performance."

I choke up regularly watching this sitcom (though in my dotage I've been known to blink back tears during long-distance carrier commercials). One scene that got me was with Pam, the receptionist-turned-saleswoman, who's gone from quiet and timorous to ambitious and occasionally acerbic.

Back when she was an aspiring artist, Pam invited the office to her student show. Only a few people come, and she overhears some of them make fun of her paintings.

She's about to leave when Michael arrives. He walks around the small space, looking at Pam's pleasant but uninspired watercolors . . . and he's amazed at her skill. Meanwhile, Fischer lets us see that while Pam's proud of her work and touched by Michael being there, somewhere inside she realizes she isn't a great artist; in fact, Michael loving her art proves it.

Then Michael comes to a small rectangular painting and his face lights up with wonder: "That's the office," he says. "That's our building. Can I buy it?" And Pam hugs him.

To get so many emotions with so few words and so much subtext . . . I can't think of a sitcom in TV history that's worked at that level.

26

Evolution Is Irritating

SITCOMS

A filmed, laugh-track-free sitcom would have been impossible to imagine just ten years ago. A viewer from the '50s or '60s would also be amazed by the way characters like *The Office*'s Pam change within the span of a season or two.

In movies or plays or novels, the main characters generally start at one point then learn and grow, ending up with a different perspective. In sitcoms, though, the characters and basic situations used to be rigorously rigid and immutable . . . for a very practical reason. The whole point of a TV series is to make one hundred episodes to sell into syndication, where they play outside of prime time, in no particular order. If characters act like us—grow or change, get new jobs, move—it confuses people watching the episodes out of order. For sitcoms, familiarity breeds contentment.

That's the genesis of the ritual happy ending that results in nothing changing, and the reason for critics' ritual complaints of artificiality—that sitcom problems are always resolved in twenty-one-minute half hours with everyone quipping incessantly and walking into homes without knocking.

Well, sure. But how about the more important ways in which sitcoms are *like* life? Most of us don't change much week to week. Mostly we find that despite great upheaval, when the dust settles our lives are pretty much the way they were before. With exceptions when our ratings are down.

Refusing to change is what humans do best, something I'll believe right up to the moment we destroy the planet. Life would be better if it were *less* like sitcoms, if we could change instantly. Evolution's all well and good, but who's got the time? When the ice caps melt, I can't wait around for gills.

Gill-call

In sitcoms, the emotional ice caps melt each week, and the characters, like us, survive by using their wits. If they succeed better than we do, it's because they have teams of highly paid, over-caffeinated writers shaping their lives.

But what is life, really, if not a very long series of twenty-one-minute half hours, renewed hour after day after year despite the doubts of our sponsor? We all have our wacky neighbors, impossible relatives, and frustrating though slightly hilarious conundrums to face each week, and they somehow get resolved, maybe not as neatly and happily as on sitcoms, but the hope that they can be is such stuff as dreams are made of.

While sitcom characters aren't the same as real people, it's none-theless a poignantly symbiotic relationship; they're idealized images of us, we're realistic versions of them. They may achieve eloquence and harmony in their lives, but they couldn't do it without the inar-ticulate messes we make of ours. They depend on us to exist, but we look to them as role models, aspiring to their wit and serendipitous resolutions.

So despair not when all seems hopelessness and confusion; some-where in Hollywood, in a room filled with nothing but imagination, M&Ms, and cocaine, there's a comedy writer shaping your anguish into a wacky subplot, your pain into a small crystalline moment of sitcom wisdom with ingenious parallel construction and alliterative hard consonants.

27

America the Hilarious

If the United States is a melting pot, it's certainly been the perfect stew for humorists; all those different races and ethnicities crammed together are primordial soup for comedy. And the races and ethnicities that are, how shall I put this, *differently* American, have been critical in providing mocking material in between when we're arresting or exploiting them.

But what is it that makes American humor so Americanishesquey?

From Trickster on, rebelling against authority has been a fundamental tenet of comedy. I've heard of a country that was *founded* on the principle of rebelling against authority.

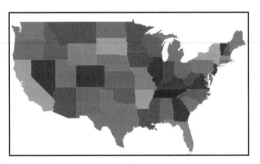

Soup

The US sees itself as a union of rugged individualists, like the nation itself is a union of individual states. Americans challenge everything; what other country's national anthem consists of almost nothing but questions? Pushing back against power, authority, restrictions—that's in the USA's DNA, so it's not surprising that it's characteristic of our most prominent comedians and comic achievements. From Chaplin and Keaton to Stiller and Ferrell, the ordinary guy who fights back is central to our comedy, and our national identity.

Even the *way* we fight back is unique. The British do it with subtlety, the French with scorn, the Italians with bombast—Americans fight back by hitting you. Where Europe sees culture, dignity, and restraint as important values, we think those things are stupid. Americans are impulsive, brash, and crude. There's nothing sly about most of our humor: it's right there, in your face, where you can't miss it, you got a problem with that?

And not just physical humor, verbal too. From "Yankee Doodle" to Mark Twain to Jay-Z, there's a Shakespearean flamboyance in the way Americans brag about themselves and trash others. We may be regular folks but we're also big and bold, like our country. Our jokes, our slapstick, our sight gags; *The Front Page*, Groucho, Lenny, Pryor— the landscape of American humor is filled with the profane, the large, and the loud, which includes the small (Chaplin, Keaton, Stiller) who get large when pushed.

Compare Keaton and a French master like Jacques Tati. The Frenchman luxuriates in nuance, creating gently unfolding labyrinthine fantasy worlds of odd noises and visual dissonance; the American charges through a chaotic world that's trying to kill him. While Tati sits on a squeaky chair, a house is falling on Buster Keaton.

Now there are some who say that America (and by implication, its identity) must soon come to terms with a reduced place in the world. Well, I think I speak for all Americans when I respond to that thoughtful, considered analysis by saying Fuck You.

Americans will never back down, from fighting or funny—there's no such thing as sit-down comedy. If we go down, we'll do it standing up—being offensive, outrageous, and out-and-out awesome. Because American comedy is nothing more, and nothing less, than America.

(With "n comedy" at the end.)

28

Kosmik Komedy 2
THE THEOLOGY OF HA!

So we can agree that we're awesome. But with a legion of people devoted to making us laugh in multiple media—TV, movies, standup, Internet, plays, books, blogs, tweets—the question (asked by me, but you have to admit that counts as it being asked) is still "How does comedy make anything better?" Well . . .

It's been said that a key purpose of art is to create a commonality of experience; what's a better example of that than shared laughter?

And laughter kills fear. Stephen Colbert: "If you're laughing, I defy you to be afraid." Even in the midst of our post-9/11 shock and horror, the satirical newspaper the *Onion* found a comedic take on terror with its headline "God Angrily Clarifies 'Don't Kill' Rule."

And killing fear allows us to grow. The Dalai Lama told John Cleese that when you laugh, it's easier to take in new ideas. Russian philosopher Mikhail Bakhtin: "Laughter demolishes fear and piety before an object, before a world, thus allowing for a free investigation of it."

Freedom is the core of comedy; by inspiring unconventional thought patterns, humor reveals hidden possibilities. John Morreall: "Part of our delight in this use of our imagination is the feeling of liberation it brings."

So comedy makes you brilliant, rich, immortal, fearless, free, and is the basis for all human knowledge. But wait, there's more!

Sam Harris, bestselling author on atheism: "Love entails the loss, to some degree, of our self-absorption." I think the same is true of comedy; for the moment we're laughing, we're out of ourselves.

Hey, wait a minute—transcending the self, negation of ego . . . that's religious talk. Loss of ego is a primary tenet of Buddhism, which

Funny

thinks so much of comedy that its logo is a laughing, half-naked fat guy.

In connecting us to others, freeing us from fear and inspiring our imagination, laughter has a spiritual power, which makes it dangerous; Freud said, "Humor is not resigned, it is rebellious." Although British comedian Peter Cook talked about "those wonderful Berlin cabarets that did so much to stop the rise of Hitler," humor *can* affect society—just ask the victims of Hipponax's satires on page 47.* It's been said that the entire ancient tradition of heraldic chivalry died on Don Quixote's lance. If comedy is powerless, why do all dictators ban satire? (At least the smart ones do; Otpur!, a Serbian resistance movement of the late '90s, helped overthrow dictator Slobodan Milosevic using street theater and pranks inspired by *Monty Python's Flying Circus*.)

Comedy = God?

Laughter's spiritual and societal power returns us to Trickster, who wasn't just a jester, remember, but for some cultures a pathway to

---

* Or the pedestrians of Bogota, where the mayor hired professional mimes to mock people who didn't follow crossing rules. And how great is it that the mayor's name was Antanus Mockus.

transcendence (page 9—pay attention!) So how do Trickster characteristics like surprise, nonsense, being mischievous, play a role in the sacred?

Religious mystics talk about "spiritual ecstasy," which begins with a sudden, unexpected revelation. Remember everyone's first comedy routine—what's the point of "Peekaboo"? Surprise, which could be defined as . . . a sudden, unexpected revelation.

Now, remember our need to find patterns or meanings in everything (pp. 117–118)? Well . . .

☞ The sacred is mystery; so is nonsense.

☞ The mind perceives nonsense/mystery as a threat and instinctively tries to solve/negate it by finding its hidden pattern.

☞ Finding the pattern/solution—or accepting that the nonsense/mystery is unsolvable—results in a moment of transcendence. It may be spiritual ecstasy (faith); but it may be laughter.

☞ A laugh, then, is a miniature ecstatic epiphany.

☞ So a way to transcendence . . . a way to the divine . . . is to get the joke.*

If that's true, then every titter is a tiny taste of transcendence; every giggle a glancing glimpse of God.

It's Funny 'Cause It's True

Clearly, comedy is a direct route to divinity. Except when it leads to damnation.

In 1983, *The Name of the Rose* was an unlikely bestseller, a medieval monastery murder mystery by Umberto Eco, an Italian semiotician (the profession of the *DaVinci Code* hero). The solution to the book's

---

* Danish philosophers with imposing names agree with me. Sören Kierkegaard: "Humor is the last stage of existential awareness before faith."

mystery (Spoiler Alert!) is that an evil abbot (with no Costello) has come into possession of the legendary lost second book of Aristotle's *Poetics*, about comedy. Because the abbot thinks laughter is heresy, he hides the book, poisoning its pages so that anyone who finds and attempts to read it will die.

In fact, some early monastic orders were like Plato's Republic—humor was forbidden.* Why?

A central question of *Rose* is whether Jesus laughed. One monk says the idea itself is sacrilegious—comedy is a sin, because if we can laugh at authority, we can laugh at God. Indeed, Trickster often mocks supernatural spirits, seeing them not as forces to be worshipped but obstacles, like the strictures of society, to be overcome.

So the evil abbot has good cause to ban humor:

Laughter frees the villain from fear of the Devil, because in the feast of fools the Devil appears poor and foolish, and therefore control-lable . . . [Laughter can] destroy death through redemption from fear. And what would we be, we sinful creatures, without fear?

The good monk answers:

[Then] perhaps the mission of those who love mankind is to make people laugh at the truth.

Truth? Someone farts and we laugh. Cameron Diaz gets semen in her hair and we laugh. A slumdog jumps into a pool of shit and we laugh.

Which Brings Us to the Ultimate Question . . .

Why are farts funny?

---

* The Rule of St. Benedict condemned "words that provoke laughter."

No, really—why? Is it the noise? Would we giggle if they sounded like wind chimes? Hard to say (though what a delightful concept, huh?), but as butt-trumpets, they're both hilarious and gross.

Maybe it's because farts come out of the body. But then why aren't tears gross? What's the difference between tears and snot? (I'm proud to say this is one of the few books you'll read this year which asks that question.)

Tears spring from emotion: from the brain and the heart, not just the body. Farting, shitting; hunger, lust; injury, disease, and the thousand (or so) natural shocks that flesh is heir to—they all expose our underlying animal nature, and how the soul is corrupted by the body's needs. (Woody Allen may be right that the heart wants what it wants, but the loins usually *get* what they want.)

Humans are miracles: we can think, create, love . . . but we're also really gross. That's funny because as much we like to believe we can transcend our animal natures, history—from *Homeric Hymn to Hermes* to *Bridesmaids*—says we can't.

If we could accept what we really are, maybe we'd all be Le Petomane's audience, wildly weeping at those wondrous wafts of wind. Instead, we're Elvis's audience on page 11, giggling with embarrassment at seeing our true bestial selves. Farts, snot, semen, vomit, shit—all those precious bodily fluids (to quote the movie *Dr. Strangelove*) remind us that, despite our pretensions, we're nothing but naked apes, impossibly far from God.

Punchline

Ancient Greek theater festivals, dominated by tragedies, always ended with a satyr play—essentially an early form of burlesque, glorying in drunkenness, broad physical comedy, and scandalous sexuality. (Aeschylus wrote one that had a satyr being masturbated by a baby.)

Why conclude a solemn spectacle with low humor? Nietzsche speculated that the satyr plays' riotous uproar provided "metaphysical

solace," that after all the doom and gloom, "life is at bottom indestruc-
tibly joyous and powerful, as expressed through beings of nature who
dwell behind all civilization and preserve their identity through every
historical movement": Tricksters, comedians—tricking and tickling,
challenging all boundaries and beliefs, reveling in humanity's hopeless
hopes and unfailing failings.

Because at our core, we're all pathetic, noble, ridiculous, yearning,
fragile creatures, mechanically repeating our farcical mistakes, slaves
to our animal appetites and body functions . . . farting and fucking
our lives away. And to what end?

Death. The punchline. The biggest joke of all.

Punchline

"Alas, poor Yorick," says Hamlet as he sees graphic proof that
behind the jester's laugh is a grinning skull. Alas, poor us. "You
live and learn," someone said to
Noel Coward, who responded,
"Then you die and forget it all."

The secret of comedy is that
it's about death—about mocking death.

Tragedy reminds us that if not
for our flaws, we could be strong,
principled, and heroic. Comedy
celebrates what we are—weak,
corrupt, and frightened . . . but raucously, outrageously alive.

*Guy goes to a doctor, doctor says, "You're gonna die." "My god! How
long do I have?" "10." "10 what?"*

"10 what?," that is the question. And the answer is "9, 8" . . . the
clock started when we were born. We know we're doomed and that's
why we're laughing.

When you look at the sweat and semen and vaginal fluids we come from, and the debased dirt and malodorous muck we're going to (or ferocious furnace flames, your choice) . . .

When you honestly face our utter helplessness and our inevitable doom . . .

What can you do except laugh or cry?

I choose laugh.

29

That's All, Folks!

Well, I hope you've learned a few things, had a few MEEs (Miniature Ecstatic Epiphanies™ © This is so totally mine), and perhaps been inspired to explore further, keeping in mind that I produced an animated series called *Duckman*, the box set is $49.95, and three cents of every sale goes to me.

As comedian Martin Mull used to say, if you've enjoyed our time together half as much as I have, then I've enjoyed it twice as much as you.

Thank you, good night, and remember your waitress.

LINKS

Access video and audio clips through www.funnythebook.com/links.
Note that videos often disappear from the Internet; if and when these
do, find them by searching with the title and/or performer. I also urge
you to get the full works to appreciate the excerpts in context.

1. "It's a Cat (Flushing the Toilet)"—Parry Gripp
2. "The 2000 Year Old Man"—Carl Reiner and Mel Brooks
3. "Hound Dog"—Elvis Presley on *The Milton Berle Show*
4. *The Kid Brother*—Harold Lloyd
5. *Duck Soup*: "Firefly's Entrance"—The Marx Brothers
6. *Duck Soup*: "The Mirror Scene"—The Marx Brothers
7. *A Night at the Opera*: "The Stateroom Scene"—The Marx Brothers
8. "The Nazz"—Lord Buckley
9. "Christ and Moses"—Lenny Bruce
10. "Why, Lord?"—Godfrey Cambridge
11. *Richard Pryor Live In Concert*: "Heart Attack"
12. *His Girl Friday*—Cary Grant, Rosalind Russell, Ralph Bellamy
13. "The Sex Life of the Polyp"—Robert Benchley
14. *A Thousand Clowns*—Jason Robards, Barbara Harris, William
    Daniels
15. "Half-Horse, Half-Alligator"—William Mooney

16. "Who's on First"—Abbott & Costello
17. *Woody Allen, Standup Comic*: "Kidnapped"
18. "Mr. Big"—Woody Allen
19. Steve Martin on *Saturday Night Live* (montage)
20. *Monty Python Live At The Hollywood Bowl*: "Ribaldry: The Dispatch of an Edible Missile"
21. *Monty Python's Life of Brian*: "Biggus Dickus"
22. *Mork and Mindy*: "Registering an Alien"—Robin Williams
23. *A Shot in the Dark*: "Billiard Cues"—Peter Sellers, George Sanders, Maurice Kaufmann
24. *The General*: "Train"—directed by Buster Keaton
25. *The Balloonatic*: "Balloon; Canoe"—Buster Keaton
26. *Steamboat Bill Jr.*: "House"—Buster Keaton
27. *Sherlock, Jr.*: "In the Movie"—Buster Keaton
28. *Sherlock, Jr.*: "Peddler"—Buster Keaton
29. *Sherlock, Jr.*: "Woman"—Buster Keaton
30. *Seven Chances*: "Rocks"—Buster Keaton
31. *The Office*: "Suggestion Box"—Steve Carell and the cast
32. *The Office*: "Halloween": Steve Carell, Jenna Fischer

MEDIAGRAPHY

INTRODUCTION

Ron Graham: "Great Genius and Profound Stupidity" (documentary: math)

Parry Gripp: "It's a Cat (Flushing The Toilet)" (YouTube)

E.B. White: "Some Remarks on Humor"; *A Subtreasury of American Humor*

CHAPTER 1

Richard Boston: *An Anatomy of Laughter* (laughter as primitive)

Henry Louis Gates Jr.: *Figures In Black: Words, Signs and the 'Racial' Self*

Rivkah Harris, summarized by John Maier in *Gilgamesh: A Reader*

Lewis Hyde: *Trickster Makes This World: Mischief, Myth and Art*; *The Gift* (Trickster, "Homeric Hymn")

Carl Jung: *Archetypes and the Collective Unconscious*

Karl Kerenyi: "The Trickster in Relation to Greek Mythology"; (in Radin—see below) (ancient drag)

Francois Lissarrague: *Greek Vases: The Athenians and Their Images*; "Sexual Life of the Satyrs," *Before Sexuality* (D.M. Halperin, J.J. Winkler, F.I. Zeitlin, ed.'s)

Dr. Paul McDonald, University of Wolverhampton (Dave Historical Humour Study)

Philip Metman: "The Trickster Figure In Schizophrenia"; *Journal of Analytical Psychology*, Vol. III Issue 1

"Monty Python: Almost The Truth" (documentary: Elvis & the "Holy Grail")

Daniel Nester: *How To Be Inappropriate* (ancient mooning)

Plato: *The Symposium* (translation, Benjamin Jowett)

Andrew Post: "Gender and Comedy" (unpublished paper)

Elvis Presley: "(You Ain't Nothin' But A) Hound Dog" ("The Milton Berle Show")

Paul Radin: *The Trickster: A Study in Native American Mythology* (sacred/profane)

Carl Reiner and Mel Brooks: "The 2000-Year-Old Man"

C.W. Spinks: "The Laughter of Signs: Semiosis as Trickster"; *Semiosis, Marginal Signs and Trickster*

CHAPTER 2

Harold Lloyd: "The Kid Brother"

CHAPTER 3

The Marx Brothers: "Duck Soup," "A Night at the Opera"

Timothy D. Noakes: *Lore of Running* (Groucho walk)

CHAPTER 4

Richard Boston: *An Anatomy of Laughter* (jester/joker)

CHAPTER 5

Lenny Bruce: "Christ and Moses"

Lord Buckley: "The Nazz"

Godfrey Cambridge: "Why, Lord?"

CHAPTER 6

Billy Grundfest: "Richard Pryor: I Ain't Dead Yet, #*%$#@!!" (documentary: D.L. Hughley)

Richard Pryor: "Heart Attack"; "Richard Pryor Live In Concert"

CHAPTER 7

Aristotle: *Poetics*

Hugh Chisholm, ed.: *Encyclopædia Britannica*, 11th ed. (Goliards)

Horace: *The Satires*

Neil MacFarquahar: "Social Media Help Keep the Door Open to Sustained Dissent Inside Saudi Arabia"; The New York Times, June 2011 (LOL)

Plato: *The Republic*

Donald Ward: *The Poets and Poetry of the Indo-Europeans* (killer satirical songs)

CHAPTER 8

Ben Hecht: *Child of the Century*

Ben Hecht, Charles MacArthur: "The Front Page," "His Girl Friday"

CHAPTER 9

Robert Benchley: "The Rope Trick Explained," "The Sex Life of the Polyp"

Benjamin Franklin: "The Grand Leap of the Whale"; *The Writings of Benjamin Franklin, Volume III: London, 1757 - 1775*

Joseph Heller: *Catch-22*

Dorothy Parker: *"Résumé"*

S.J. Perelman: *"Strictly From Hunger"*

CHAPTER 10

Mary Chase: "Harvey"

Herb Gardner: "A Thousand Clowns"

CHAPTER 11

Bud Abbott & Lou Costello: "Who's On First"

Ricky Jay: *Learned Pigs and Fireproof Women*

Mark Twain: "Half-horse, Half-alligator"; *Life On The Mississippi* (adapted by William Mooney)

The Marx Brothers: "A Day At The Races"

CHAPTER 12

Joseph Berger: "At 100, Still a Teacher, and Quite a Character"; *The New York Times* (Bel Kaufman); May 2011

Sigmund Freud: *Jokes and their Relation to the Unconscious*

Michael Kantor, Laurence Maslon, Jon Macks: "Make 'Em Laugh" (documentary: Mel Brooks—Jews)

Brian Posehn: "Wowschwitz" ("The Sarah Silverman Program")

Joseph Telushkin: *Jewish Humor*

Time Magazine: "Analyzing Jewish Comics"; October 1978 (percentage of Jewish comics)

CHAPTER 13

Woody Allen: "Kidnapped," "The Kugelmass Episode," "Men of Crisis: The Harvey Wallinger Story" (unaired PBS special), "Mr. Big," "My Speech To The Graduates," "Vodka Ad," "The Whore of Mensa"

Douglas Brode: *Woody Allen: His Films and Career* (public performance/private confession)

CHAPTER 14

Samuel Beckett: *The Complete Works*

CHAPTER 15

Jimmy Carr & Lucy Greeves: *The Naked Jape* (Early Man threat-response; see also V.S. Ramachandran, Sandra Blakeslee: *Phantoms In The Brain*)

Matthew Hurley, Daniel Dennett, Reginald Adams Jr.: "Inside Jokes: Using Humor to Reverse-Engineer the Mind" (cognitive prowess)

David Lloyd: "Chuckles Bites The Dust" ("The Mary Tyler Moore Show")

Stephen Potter: *The Sense of Humour*

V.S. Ramachandran: "The Neurology and Evolution of Humor, Laughter and Smiling: The False Alarm Theory"; *Medical Hypotheses*, Vol. 51, Issue 4 (needle-jab laughter)

Albert Rapp: *The Origins of Wit and Humor* (roar of triumph)

Mark Singer: "Pacing It"; *The New Yorker*, March 2011 (Stoppard)

CHAPTER 16

Christian Charles, Jerry Seinfeld: "Comedian" (documentary: Glenn Miller)

Arthur Koestler: *The Act of Creation*

Steve Martin: *Born Standing Up: A Comic's Life*, "Saturday Night Live"

CHAPTER 17

Mark Beeman, Karuna Subramaniam in Benedict Carey: "Tracing the Spark of Creative Problem-Solving," *The New York Times*, Dec. 2010 (humor and learning)

Lee Berk, Stanley Tan: "The Laughter-Immune Connection"; *Humor and Health Journal*, Sept./Oct. 1996

Huntington Brown: *Rabelais in English Literature* (deadly laughter)

Alastair Clarke: *The Pattern Recognition Theory of Humour*

Norman Cousins: *Anatomy of an Illness as Perceived by the Patient: Reflections on Healing and Regeneration*

The Daily Mail: "Man Dies Laughing at The Goodies" (deadly laughter)

R.I.M. Dunbar, Rebecca Baron, Anna Frangou, Eiluned Pearce, Edwin J.C. van Leeuwin, Julie Stow, Giselle Partridge, Ian MacDonald, Vincent Barra and Mark van Vugt: "Social laughter is correlated with an elevated pain threshold"; *Proceedings of the Royal Society B* (online), Sept. 2011

Shevack Friedler et. al: "The effect of medical clowning on pregnancy rates after in vitro fertilization and embryo transfer"; *Fertility & Sterility*, Jan. 2011

W.F. Fry: "The physiologic effects of humor, mirth, and laughter"; *Journal of the American Medical Association*, April 1992 (child laughter, rowing)

Matthew M. Hurley, Daniel C. Dennett, Reginald B. Adams, Jr.: *Inside Jokes: Using Humor To Reverse-Engineer The Mind* (humor as brain-bribe)

Dr. Madan Kataria: Laughter Yoga International (website)

John Lahr: "Master of Revels"; *The New Yorker*, May 2010 (deadly laughter)

Jonah Lehrer: *How We Decide* (dopamine)

Leo Lewis: "Why Japan is laughing all the way to the bank"; *The Times of London*, Oct. 2007

Richard Mulcaster: *Positions Concerning the Training Up of Children* (16th-century laughter cure)

Jaak Pankseppa, Jeff Burgdorf: "'Laughing' rats and the evolutionary antecedents of human joy?"; *Physiology & Behavior*, fall 2006

Monty Python: "Ribaldry: The Dispatch of an Edible Missile" ("Monty Python Live At The Hollywood Bowl"), "Monty Python's Life of Brian"

Andrew Post: "Gender and Comedy" (unpublished paper)

Travis Proulx and Steven J. Heine: "Connections From Kafka: Exposure to Meaning Threats Improves Implicit Learning of an Artificial Grammar"; *Psychological Science*, Jan. 2000 (nonsense & I.Q.)

Robert Provine: *Laughter: A Scientific Investigation* (laughter epidemic, everyday laughter)

V.S. Ramachandran: "The Neurology and Evolution of Humor, Laughter and Smiling: The False Alarm Theory"; *Medical Hypotheses*, Vol. 51, Issue 4 (smiling)

Brent A. Scott, Christopher M. Barnes: "A Multilevel Field Investigation of Emotional Labor, Affect, Work Withdrawal, and Gender"; *Academy of Management Journal*, Feb. 2011 (fake smiling)

Robert Tait: "Laugh, I nearly went to Tehran! Iranian capital starts laughing classes"; *The Guardian*, Nov. 2009

Lawrence Weschler: *A Miracle, A Universe: Settling Accounts with Torturers* (laughter as torture)

CHAPTER 19

Edward de Bono: *The Mechanism of Mind* (pattern recognition)

Buster Keaton: "The Blacksmith," "The General"

Rouben Mamoulian, Greta Garbo: "Queen Christina"

Paul McGhee: *Humor: Its Origins and Development* (humor/beauty)

Peter Sellers, Blake Edwards: "A Shot In The Dark"

William Shakespeare: "Love's Labors Lost"

Mikhail Yampolsky: "Kuleshov's Experiments and the New Anthropology of the Actor" in Richard Taylor and Ian Christie, ed.: "Inside the Film Factory: New Approaches to Russian and Soviet Cinema"

CHAPTER 20

Henry Beard, Christopher Cerf: "Americans United To Beat The Dutch"; *The National Lampoon*, April 1973

Agatha Christie: "The Murder of Roger Ackroyd"

Sigmund Freud: *Jokes and their Relation to the Unconscious*

Richard Wiseman, University of Hertfordshire; "LaughLab" (www. laughlab.co.uk/)

Steven Levy: "Does Your iPod Play Favorites?"; *Newsweek*, Jan. 2005 (randomness)

CHAPTER 21

Jorge Luis Borges: "Pierre Monard, Author of The Quixote"

Daily Mail Online: "Cheeky monkey! Macaque borrows photographer's camera to take hilarious self-portraits"; July 2011

Jonathan Lethem: "The Ecstasy of Influence: A Plagiarism"; *Harper's Magazine*, Feb. 2007

CHAPTER 22
Brigitte Berman: "Hugh Hefner: Playboy, Activist and Rebel" (documentary)
Henri Bergson: *Laughter: An Essay on the Meaning of the Comic* (animal/mechanical)
Sigmund Freud: *Jokes and their Relation to the Unconscious*
Elena Gorokhova: *A Mountain of Crumbs* (butcher joke)
Thomas Hobbes: *Elements of Law* (superiority theory)
Jan Walsh Hokenson: *The Idea of Comedy: History, Theory, Critique* (Plato/desires)
Immanuel Kant: *Critique of Pure Reason* (Incongruity Theory)
Buster Keaton: "The Balloonatic"
Walter Kerr: *The Silent Clowns*
Arthur Koestler: *The Act of Creation*
Robert L. Latta: *The Basic Humor Process: A Cognitive-Shift Theory and the Case Against Incongruity (Humor Research No. 5)*
John Morreall: *Taking Laughter Seriously*
Octavio Paz: *The Double Flame*
Herbert Spencer: "The Physiology of Laughter"; *MacMillan's Magazine*, March 1860

CHAPTER 23
Penelope Gilliatt: "Buster Keaton"; *The National Society of Film Critics on Movie Comedy* ("Never beg")
Buster Keaton: "College," "A Funny Thing Happened To Me On The Way To The Forum," "The General," "The Playhouse," "Seven Chances," "Sherlock Jr.," "A Southern Yankee," "Steamboat Bill Jr."
David Robinson: *Keaton*

CHAPTER 24

Phil Austin: "The Regional American Surrealist Cookbook" (website: "The Big Jewel")

Lord Byron: *"Don Juan"*

Lawrence Ferlinghetti: "Triumph of the Postmodern"

William Hazlitt: *On Wit and Humour*

Carl Jung: *Archetypes and the Collective Unconscious*

Michael Kantor, Laurence Maslon, Jon Macks: "Make 'Em Laugh" (documentary; Michael McKean)

Wendy Keys: "Milton Glaser: To Inform and Delight" (documentary)

Louis Kronenberger: *The Thread of Laughter: Chapters on English Stage Comedy from Jonson to Maugham*

John Lahr: "Mouth to Mouth" (*The New Yorker*, May 2011) (Sarah Ruhl)

H.L. Mencken: *A Book of Burlesques*

CHAPTER 25

Greg Daniels: "Halloween" ("The Office")

Larry Wilmore: "Performance Review" ("The Office")

CHAPTER 27

"Make 'Em Laugh" (documentary; America as primordial soup)

CHAPTER 28

Mikhail Bakhtin: *Dialogic Imagination* (laughter vs. fear)

María Cristina Caballero: "Academic Turns City Into A Social Experiment"; *Harvard Gazette*, March 2004 (Bogata traffic mimes)

Stephen Colbert: *Parade*, Sept. 2007

Umberto Eco: *The Name of the Rose*

Sam Harris: *The End of Faith*

Emily Lutzker: "Anxiety and Whimsy In Popular Culture" (unpublished doctoral dissertation; European Graduate School)

John Morreall: *Taking Laughter Seriously*

Friedrich Nietzsche: *The Birth of Tragedy*

Alleen Pace Nilson, Don L.F. Nilsen: *Encylopedia of 20th-Century American Humor* (Cleese/Dalai Lama)

I.M. Resnick: "'Risus monasticus': Laughter and Medieval Monastic Culture"; *Revue Benedictine 97*

Mac Linscott Ricketts: "The Structure and Religious Significance of the Trickster-Transformer-Culture Hero in the Mythology of the North American Indians"—doctoral dissertation, University of Chicago (Trickster mocking)

Tina Rosenberg: "Revolution U: What Egypt Learned from the Students Who Overthrew Milosevic"; *Foreign Policy*, Feb. 2011

SOURCES

"While in India": Benchley, Robert, *My Ten Years in a Quandry, and How They Grew*, New York, 1936.

"Have a bit of the wing": Perelman, S.J., *Strictly From Hunger*, New York, 1937.

"Just what the hell": Heller, Joseph, *Catch-22*, New York, 1961.

"I am not an exceptional man": Gardner, Herb, *A Thousand Clowns*, New York, 1962.

"And I said 'No'": Allen, Woody, "The Vodka Ad"

"An ability to recognize patterns": Clarke, Alastair, *The Pattern Recognition Theory of Humour*, Cumbria, 2008.

"I read a treatise on comedy": Martin, Steve, *Born Standing Up: A Comic's Life*, New York, 2007.

"I made the joyous discovery": Cousins, Norman, *Anatomy of an Illness as Perceived by the Patient: Reflections on Healing and Regeneration*, New York, 1979.

"Laughter frees the villein": Eco, Umberto, *The Name of the Rose*, Boston 1983.

PHOTO CREDITS

Grateful acknowledgment is made to the following for permission to use images.

Associated Press: 41, 77, 86
cliff1066: 68
David Hume Kennedy/Gerald R. Ford Presidential Library: 129
Everett Collection: 103
Glen Anderson: 153
Graphics Factory CC: 165
iStockphoto: 100, 168
Jason Wiede: 127
John Tenniel: 112
Library of Congress: 16, 52, 53, 58, 129
Mark DiTKon: 127
Mitchell Hasseth / © NBC Universal, Inc./: 155
Mr. Misch's 70's House of Turtlenecks & Suede: 108
National Park Service; photo by T. Rains: 162
New York World-Telegram and the Sun Newspaper Photograph Collection, Library of Congress: 11
Photofest: 22, 34, 59, 64, 65, 69, 72, 76, 93, 106, 114, 119, 135, 139, 149, 172

Reuvenk: 73

Ricardo André Frantz: 30

Robert Provine, originally published in *American Scientist*: 1

Stefan Reicheneder: 117

Stefan Scheer, courtesy of Stefanie Krull, Neanderthal Museum, Mettmann, Germany: 6

Superstock: 146

Every reasonable effort has been made to contact copyright holders and secure permissions. Omissions can be remedied in future editions.

INDEX

ABOUT THE AUTHOR

The beginnings of David Misch are clouded in mystery and legend and stuff. No one currently alive knows exactly how (or why) Misch entered the world of writing, when he acquired the dueling scar that forced him to purchase those now-famous prosthetic eyebrows, or where he left his tennis socks.

One version of his story says he was a standup named Best Comedian in Boston by *Boston Magazine* and that his song "Somerville" was released nationally by Fretless Records. Then, through a strange series of events involving a warehouse filled with industrial diamonds, a woman in an ocelot costume, and the prime minister of England, he was hired to write for the Emmy-winning *Mork and Mindy* and the Emmy-losing *Police Squad!*

As the years rushed by in a phantasmagorical (and, one can assume, pharmacological) haze, it's said that David wrote and/or produced pilots for NBC (David Letterman's first talk show), CBS, ABC, Fox, UPN, HBO, Showtime, PBS, ABC Family, Disney, Universal, and Lifetime. He produced series for CBS (*Take Five*), USA (*Duckman*), national syndication (*She Spies*), and was a guest writer on *Saturday Night Live*. His work has been nominated for multiple Emmys and won the CableACE and Banff International Television awards. In features, he sold a number of screenplays (note: "sold" not "got produced") and was special consultant on *The Muppets Take Manhattan.*

David wrote the book for *Hip Pocket Musicals*, which was presented at Pepsico Summerfare (SUNY, Purchase) and has had one-act plays produced in Los Angeles and New York. As of this writing, his play *Occupied* is scheduled to be produced by the Katselas Theatre Company in Los Angeles, but you know theater.

David's prose has been featured on NationalLampoon.com, collected in the anthology *May Contain Nuts* (Harper Perennial), and he blogs for the *Huffington Post*. He's lectured and taught at various gullible institutions, including the Skirball Cultural Center, UCLA's Herb Alpert School of Music, and USC's School of Cinematic Arts.

David's wife, Dr. Amy Gelfand, is a family physician; their daughter, Emily Misch, is an opera singer.